RAISING
PROPHETS
& PROPHETIC TYPES

UNLOCKING THEIR SUPERNATURAL GIFTS

D'ANDREA BOLDEN

Bolden Publishing

D'Andrea M. Bolden

Unless otherwise indicated, all scriptural quotations are from the *King James Version* of the Bible.

Raising Prophets & Prophetic Types:
Unlocking Their Supernatural Gifts
Written by D'Andrea Bolden

Published by
Bolden Publishing
P.O. Box 2025
Kalamazoo, MI 49003
boldenenterprisesllc@gmail.com

Reproduction of text in whole or in part without the written consent by the author is not permitted and is unlawful according to the 1976 United States Copyright Act.

Cover design and book production by:
Bolden Publishing

Cover illustration is protected by the 1976 United States Copyright Act.

Copyright © 2019, 2016 by D'Andrea Bolden
All Rights Reserved

Library of Congress of Cataloging-in Publication Data:
An application to Register this book for cataloging has been submitted to the Library of Congress

2nd Edition

Printed in the United States of America

D'Andrea M. Bolden

Foreword

There is a great need for teachings, trainings and ministers that focus on the discipleship and spiritual growth of our children. They are literally our future and the next generation to carry the torch. There are a lot of books that are geared towards adults but this book is truly like none other.

The revelation and insight within the pages of this book is fresh and thought-provoking. It is a blessing to have a book full of wisdom about prophetic children for they have many of the same capabilities as adults. One of the most neglected yet fruitful and rewarding ministries is that of ministering to children.

It is time for believers worldwide to rise up to the occasion and challenge of cultivating and developing our children in order to disciple them and help them to mature spiritually.

- **Apostle Ralph Cunningham-M.A., LLPC, ADA**

D'Andrea M. Bolden

Table of Contents

Section 1 – Raising Prophets + Prophetic Types
Introduction [Pg. 2]
Chapter 1 - A child is Born [Pg. 8]
Chapter 2 - Love, Encouragement, & ... [Pg. 11]
Chapter 3 - Matter of the Heart [Pg. 14]
Chapter 4 - Budding Personality [Pg. 21]
Chapter 5 - Guard Them [Pg. 24]
Chapter 6 - Footsteps to Follow [Pg. 30]
Chapter 7 - Growing in Grace [Pg. 33]
Chapter 8 - Identifying Gifts & Talents [Pg. 35]
Chapter 9 - God Speaks to Children – [Pg. 40]
Chapter 10 - Identifying + Breaking Generational Curses [Pg. 44]
Chapter 11 - Balancing it Out [Pg. 53]
Chapter 12 - Prophetic Stirring [Pg. 56]
Chapter 13 - Prophetic Gifted Children [Pg. 63]
Chapter 14 - Deliverance and Children [Pg. 69]
Chapter 15 - Prayers, Declarations and Decrees [Pg. 75]
Chapter 16 - Purpose Driven Parenting [Pg. 81]
Chapter 17 - Personal Development Plan Template [Pg. 84]
Chapter 18 – Activations [Pg. 86]
Conclusion [Pg. 96]

Section 2 – Young Prophetic Artists: God's Forgotten Creatives
Introduction [Pg. 98]
Chapter 1 - Art & Creativity [Pg. 100]
Chapter 2 - God's Forgotten Creatives [Pg. 104]
Chapter 3 - Prophetic Expression [Pg. 111]
Chapter 4 - Prophetic Flow [Pg. 113]
Chapter 5 - Prophetic Artists [Pg. 115]
Conclusion [Pg. 120]

Section 3 - Dreams, Visions + Supernatural Encounters
Introduction [Pg. 122]
Chapter 1 - The Language of God [Pg. 124]
Chapter 2 - Dreams [Pg. 135]

Chapter 3 - Visions [Pg. 139]
Chapter 4 - Special Communication to Special People [Pg. 141]
Chapter 5- Supernatural Encounters [Pg. 145]
Chapter 6- Tips and Tools for Dreams [Pg. 148]
Parent & Kid Devotion Day 1 [Pg. 151]
Parent & Kid Devotion Day 2 [Pg. 153]
Parent & Kid Devotion Day 3 [Pg. 156]
Parent & Kid Devotion Day 4 [Pg. 157]
Parent & Kid Devotion Day 5 [Pg. 160]

Section 4- Innovators, Inventors + Entrepreneurs

Chapter 1 – Innovation [pg. 162]
Chapter 2 – Inventions + Dream [pg. 164]
Chapter 3 – Entrepreneurship [pg. 168]

Section 5- Bright Idea

Bright Idea – Brainstorming [pg.172]
Bright Idea- Invention [pg. 173]
Bright Idea – Business Idea [pg.175]
Bright Idea – Other Idea [pg. 177]
Bright Idea – Action Steps Introduction [pg. 179]
Bright Idea – Action Steps [pg. 180]

Section 6- Dream Journal

Dream Journal [183-218]

D'Andrea M. Bolden

Section 1

Raising Prophets + Prophetic Types

D'Andrea M. Bolden

Introduction

There are many books, blogs, CD's, DVD's and other resources that emphasize discipleship and spiritual growth in adults. However, there aren't many resources available for children. When people think of children and church, many times they only think of songs and games. We should not overlook the fact that children are indeed spiritual giants in their own right. Jesus adores and loves the little children but, in some cases, we wait until precious developmental years are long gone before we emphasize the fullness of a relationship with God and discovering their identity and purpose in Christ Jesus.

> **Matthew 19:14"** Jesus said, "Let the little children come to me, and do not hinder them, for the kingdom of heaven belongs to such as these."(NIV)

Cultivate: [1]To promote or improve the growth of by labor or attention.

Cultivate: [2] To develop or improve by education or training

Develop: [1]To cause to grow or expand

Develop: [2]To bring out the capabilities or possibilities of; bring to a more advanced or effective state.

Discipleship: The process of becoming learned in order to embrace and assist in spreading the teachings of Jesus Christ.

As parents we have the power to cause our children to grow spiritually because of our labor and attention (cultivate). We also have the opportunity to bring out the best in our children (develop). We play such a powerful role in the lives of our children and have been given the charge to cultivate and develop our children. It is our responsibility to teach our children the Word of God that they may become disciples or one's that are learned in the teachings of Jesus Christ. In other words, that they will simply but powerfully follow Him. In order to learn anything and become efficient it takes discipline. So, we can say that discipline and discipleship walk hand in hand. If Jesus took the time to teach and train his disciples in around 3 years how much more can we do with a child from birth through early adulthood.

In order for a farmer to have a great harvest and healthy crops it takes the attention and skill of the laborers to ensure maximum results and a plentiful harvest. Parents and guardians alike can apply that same concept to our children. The effort we put in from day one can eventually manifest as a great reward once we can see the fruit of our labor when our children grow up to be well-rounded productive individuals who serve the Lord in gladness.

> **Psalm 127:3**" Children are a heritage from the LORD, offspring a reward from him." (NIV)

Summary of Developmental Stages

Below is a brief overview of the stages of childhood development according to the model outlined by Erik Erikson. Under each age range, there are notes that correspond, but children mature at different rates. Therefore, some may be more advanced or even develop at a slower rate. These are some basic and obviously not exhaustive concepts for each developmental stage. Although the Erik Erikson model goes all the way through adulthood for the purposes of this book, I just wanted to share that which is applicable to children.

> **Deuteronomy 31:13**" And that their children, which have not known any thing, may hear, and learn to fear the LORD your God, as long as ye live in the land whither ye go over Jordan to possess it." (KJV)

Infancy: Birth – 18 months

When our children are in the womb and when they are born we should seek God for their purpose as well as prophesy and speak the Word of God over their lives. God desires for us to understand the purposes He has for our children so that we can continuously speak these things and remind them for many years to come.

John The Baptist

> **Luke 1:11-17**" Then an angel of the Lord appeared to him, standing at the right side of the altar of incense. When Zechariah saw him, he was startled and was gripped with fear. But the angel said to him: "Do not be afraid, Zechariah; your prayer has been heard. Your wife Elizabeth will bear you a son, and you are to call him John. He will be a joy and delight to you, and many will rejoice because of his birth, for he will be great in the sight of the Lord. He is never to take wine or other fermented drink, and he will be

filled with the Holy Spirit even before he is born. He will bring back many of the people of Israel to the Lord their God. And he will go on before the Lord, in the spirit and power of Elijah, to turn the hearts of the parents to their children and the disobedient to the wisdom of the righteous—to make ready a people prepared for the Lord." (NIV)

The Lord made sure the parents of John the Baptist knew that there was a huge assignment for his life, and they were even given instructions in order to ensure that he stayed away from wine and strong drink.

Jesus Christ

Luke 1:27-33 "To a virgin pledged to be married to a man named Joseph, a descendant of David. The virgin's name was Mary. The angel went to her and said, "Greetings, you who are highly favored! The Lord is with you. Mary was greatly troubled at his words and wondered what kind of greeting this might be. But the angel said to her, "Do not be afraid, Mary; you have found favor with God. You will conceive and give birth to a son, and you are to call him Jesus. He will be great and will be called the Son of the Most High. The Lord God will give him the throne of his father David, and he will reign over Jacob's descendants forever; his kingdom will never end." (NIV)

The revelation of Jesus and who He is was revealed to Mary before she would carry a child. Our God is all knowing and He is more than able to reveal to us things that we know not especially as it pertains to our children. We always say children do not come with an instruction manual because they are all different; their personalities, likes and even dislikes can be extreme opposites even amongst siblings. But God has given us His Word and if we petition Him, He is more than able to give us instructions concerning our children. If my television is not working correctly, I would call the manufacturer or the company who made the television set. So, if we are unsure of the inner-workings of our children we must go to God, the one who created them.

> **Ephesians 2:10** "For we are his workmanship, created in Christ Jesus unto good works, which God hath before ordained that we should walk in them." (KJV)

Early Childhood: 2-3 years' old

During the toddler years' children are mobile and talking more and learning very quickly as they interact with their environment. This is a great time to show them how to pray and even engage in worship by lifting their hands, clapping their hands and shouting unto the Lord.

Preschool: 3-5 years' old

During the preschool years young children are growing and learning to communicate at a higher level and they can really begin to learn to pray more and memorize scriptures.

School Age: 6-11 years old

We are to keep them in the Word and although prayer is not widely allowed in school it must be and remain in our homes. This is a great age for children to learn to hear and recognize the voice of the Holy Spirit.

Adolescence: 12- 18 years old

Children should become more independent in studying the Word and praying on their own with parents to consistently reinforce this and guide them as they continue to mature. By this age they need to desire a relationship with God without being forced.

One thing that sticks out to me is that adolescence starts at the age of 12/13. This is an important age because as believers we say this age is a time when children become responsible to observe and obey the Word of God. This is also true with those who practice Judaism. The reason this age range is so important is because by the time a child becomes a teenager or adolescent, they become less pliable in a sense as they are becoming more independent and are trying to grasp their identity as an individual. In other words, once a child reaches a certain milestone, they are becoming less reliable on their parents and are more capable of making decisions on their own. Although the role of a parent never truly ends in the life of their child the way a child is handled by a parent at the age of 1, 7, or even 16 should look very different.

D'Andrea M. Bolden

A Child is Born

1

Small, precious, cuddly and adorable are common terms used to describe newborn babies. I like to use terms such as tiny agents of change, treasure box, and future kingdom ambassadors. We have to remember although small at birth these tiny people will grow up to become adults and much of their future success is up to us as guardians and parents.

One of the biggest oversights we make as Christian parents is negating the power of words. Words are like spiritual containers that frame our world. So, whether we speak words of life or death over our children is up to us. From birth through adulthood while we as parents are alive and able we have the power and opportunity to speak the Word of God, words of prophecy, life and destiny into our children.

> **Proverbs 18:20-21** "A man's belly shall be satisfied with the fruit of his mouth; and with the increase of his lips shall he be filled. Death and life are in the power of the tongue: and they that love it shall eat the fruit thereof. (KJV)

Unfortunately, many times we miss these opportunities. We can get a lot of things back in life but time is not one of them. Therefore, it is imperative that we seize the moment or take every opportunity we can to sow righteous seeds into the lives of our children that can stick with them for the rest of their lives.

> **Proverbs 22:6** "Train up a child in the way he should go: and when he is old, he will not depart from it. (KJV)

If we never take the time to teach our children who they are in God that is a prime way for ungodly influences to steer them onto a path of destruction. This path is filled with confusion and a lack of true identity. Every person in this world has a purpose and a God given assignment. As a parent we have to use the formative years to prepare them to be and do what God desired according to His good and perfect will.

Children should be seen as a ministry to the parent for the purposes of raising him/her in the fear and admonition of the Lord. We've been blessed to prepare them to be productive and responsible adults. Parents have a responsibility to equip their children as Kingdom ambassadors who are beginning to identify and understand their call and purpose in the earth. We should be teaching them the Word of God while making it applicable and relevant to their level of understanding and maturity.

Being a parent is a huge responsibility and it is also a great opportunity to disciple and train individuals. As parents we should never place the full responsibility of our children's spiritual development and growth in the hands of others. One thing that has always stuck with me is that ministry starts at home. So, before we go out to our communities, cities, and even to the nations we have to preach and teach at home in word and deed.

Many people have the misconception that if they are doing the work of the Lord that the Holy Spirit or God himself is going to raise their children. This is the reason many gifted and called children go down the wrong path. Many times, they have been neglected by parents who are putting ministry first. Yet, when we read the Word of God, we can see that family and marriage were ordained by God **before** ministry. When we look at life through a biblically correct perspective, we understand the importance of our home being in order before we pursue ministerial callings.

Love, Encouragement & Positive Reinforcement

2

Children have resilience but at the same time they are fragile and can be broken if mishandled. It is easy to break a glass bowl but very hard and nearly impossible sometimes to put it back together. As a child grows and develops, they become less pliable and more like a glass bowl. Emotional scars caused by trauma and abuse can cause a child full of potential to live an unsuccessful adult life and miss their God given calling and purpose. When children have had painful and traumatic situations transpire in their lives it is important that they receive counseling from an experienced and credentialed Christian counselor. The reason I say Christian counselor is because it is a good idea to find a professional mental health counselor that will reiterate biblical principles and beliefs. An unbelieving counselor will have a more secular humanistic approach regardless of their counseling perspective. This could potentially destroy the faith-based foundation of a child leaving them in a state of confusion and disbelief.

The love, encouragement, and positive reinforcement received from a parent or guardian can help to build a healthy personality and self-esteem in a young child. A lack of love, encouragement and positive reinforcement can be detrimental to a young child and is like poison that slowly kills godly purpose and can skew the child's perspective and belief in God.

I have personally seen how the lack of love from a natural father can cause an individual to become unable to receive the love of our Heavenly Father or even deny His very existence. Love makes an individual feel wanted and even gives one a sense of security. When a child feels and knows that they are loved they are happier and more likely to develop a healthy personality with the ability to maintain healthy relationships in the future. We must constantly reinforce the love of God to our children and let them know how much God loves them and how special they are to Him.

> **Psalm 139:14** " I will praise thee; for I am fearfully and wonderfully made: marvelous are thy works; and that my soul knoweth right well." (KJV)
>
> **John 3:16** "For God so loved the world, that he gave his only begotten Son, that whosoever believeth in him should not perish, but have everlasting life." (KJV)

Encouragement gives a child that extra push to know that they can do or be something great. Encouragement from a place of love will aid a child in being secure in his or herself. Encouragement can gently guide a young child in the right direction or persuade them to do more than they would attempt to do on their own.

Positive reinforcement is the concept of rewarding good behavior and not bad. Behavior that is rewarded is more likely to be repeated again in the future. So, when we reward or even verbally praise our children for exhibiting good behavior, they are more likely to repeat this behavior in the future.

A Matter of The Heart

<u>3</u>

Proverbs 4:23 "Keep thy heart with all diligence; for out of it are the issues of life." (KJV)

Proverbs 22:15 "Foolishness is bound in the heart of a child; but the rod of correction shall drive it far from him." (KJV)

Many adults have been raised in a Christian home that believe in spanking. Even today many Christians believe in spanking their children based on a scripture in the bible (Proverbs 13:24). Unfortunately, many of those same parents today are very reactive in their style of parenting. Meaning every time their child does or says something undesirable, they are likely to get a spanking.

Proverbs 13:24" He that spareth his rod hateth his son: but he that loveth him chasteneth him betimes." (KJV)

Proverbs 29:15" The rod and reproof give wisdom: but a child left to himself bringeth his mother to shame."

The reason most parents will say their children are spanked is because they get out of line or are disobedient. Amongst Americans as a whole a lot of people spank their children but ironically many of these same children end up living lives that cause them to end up in an early grave, in prison, or living miserable and defeated lives. Over the years as I studied for the purposes of research, I began to ponder how it was possible to lose so many children in our communities when parents are disciplining their children in line with what they feel is right according to their beliefs. It appeared that in many cases "spanking" only seemed to work for a period of time but failed to yield results that can be seen in adulthood.

Spanking a child is a form of punishment that usually will cause a child to avoid repeating the same mistake. In other words, the child will adjust or change their behavior to avoid getting another spanking. But many times, no change has taken place in their heart. So, you have children that learn how to act and behave around their parents to avoid getting in trouble, but their heart remains in the same condition. We must take the time to talk to our children and teach them and correct them in areas we see they need help. In the 23rd Psalm David said, "thy rod and thy staff they comfort me." The rod had everything to do with correction but a lot of parents can be too quick tempered or have a one-track mind in how to correct their children.

I have seen countless videos on social media where parents are literally fist fighting their children. Out of ignorance, many parents are crossing the line of abuse and beating their children into a state of anger and rage. Additionally, some are even punching, back hand slapping and violently attacking their children. Parents get furious that a child will not obey or is disrespectful or is continuing to break rules with no signs of stopping. One thing I was always taught by my father is that my hands are to be used to pray for my children and bless them and not to strike or hit them. Regardless of your personal views on spanking (corporal punishment) there is a huge difference between a spanking and blatant abuse.

When there is a lack of structure and discipline, spanking lacks effectiveness and when used in excess it will cause a child to become angry, rebellious or extremely passive. When this disciplinary style of spanking is handled incorrectly the focus is only on shaping behavior while neglecting the state and contents of the heart. In other words, many parents are just hitting kids with no structure, correction, or proper discipline in the home but are only reacting to their child's undesired behaviors. When a child is constantly in trouble for the same thing over and over there is a heart issue that needs to be dealt with.

We have to constantly be aware not just of our children's behavior but also the state of their heart. As heart issues remain neglected these things become deeply embedded into the inner workings of the child. It is imperative for parents to understand that children show how they feel differently than adults especially when they are too young to fully express themselves. For example, a depressed child can easily be mistaken or misdiagnosed because the symptoms of depression in children do not always present themselves in the same manner as adults.

When the perspective of parenting shifts, the heart of a child is dealt with and therefore the desired behaviors will follow.

The purpose of this chapter is not to be an advocate or proponent of spanking but instead to show how spanking <u>or any other form of discipline</u> without dealing with the heart of a child can lack effectiveness in the long run.

Concerns of the heart :(Hannah's Story)

I can remember years ago when my daughter Hannah was young, she began to pick at her skin to the point of bleeding. I would tell her not to do that and even discipline her, but nothing worked. Whenever she could not get her way, she would pick her skin. She also did this when she was mad or when lying down late at night. I would get so frustrated and angry as a parent because I did not know what to do about this situation. I purchased stress balls for her to squeeze instead of picking her skin but the behavior continued. I would ask her why she was doing that and her only reply would be, "I do not know." Those words would agitate me more than what she was doing at the time.

I was eventually at the point of being totally frustrated and perplexed as a parent. It seemed that I could not understand nor get through to my child so that she would comply with the situation. I felt like I was losing her and that there was no hope for things to get better. I remember feeling down because I did not want my child to begin to develop habits that would cross over into bigger issues later in life. I had a hard time handling this situation as a single mother with no help. My daughter displayed what might be considered a spirit of apathy. I could see no difference between happy, sad, mad, angry, excited and so forth. So, like any parent I prayed but nothing changed and this situation continued on with little signs of improvement.

I eventually got to my breaking point and I was absolutely fed up. Then, she finally opened her mouth and said that she was upset because she wanted to see her biological father. I would ask her all the time and she said she was fine because he had never been in her life or seen her since she was a baby. I then began to realize I was dealing with abandonment, rebellion, rejection, bitterness, and even anger. I knew it was time for me as a parent to use my authority and fight. I began to pray specifically about those areas and slowly things took a turn for the better. I also ministered deliverance to Hannah and I began to tear down Satan's kingdom that was trying to destroy my child. Today Hannah is totally free from this behavior and is a happy child that expresses herself and is enjoying her childhood.

Submitted by Hannah's mom

--------End

With stories like the aforementioned I cannot over emphasize that children due to a lack of life experience and understanding are usually unable to effectively communicate how they feel. Hannah picking at her skin all over her body was a red flag that something was wrong. Children that are separated from a parent for whatever reason will always desire to openly communicate with the absent parent or guardian. If we allow things to fester in our children once they get to a more independent age, we can find them walking on a road of destruction and rebellion because of issues that were not dealt with from years prior.

Stings of Abuse

Abuse can come in many forms such as; verbal, physical, emotional, sexual or even spiritual. But I want to take the time to focus on sexual abuse. The enemy loves to find ways to destroy people in the days of their youth. He will inflict and cause pain during an individual's childhood so that those offenses will drive them to dependence or even addiction to alcohol and drugs, prison, instability and crime sprees or just being stuck in a place of depression and brokenness. Sexual abuse, however, can come in various forms such as exploitation, oral sex, fondling, groping, kissing, sodomy, vaginal intercourse, object or digital penetration.

Sexual abuse can cause great shame, guilt and embarrassment for the victims, especially males. Abuse is hard on all victims, but males can have a tendency to become extremely aggressive and rebellious and many also express uncertainties as it pertains to sexual orientation. There is a falsehood that causes males to feel more embarrassed than females as it relates to sexual abuse. The sense of being stripped of their "manhood" or being less of a man is a common battle and thought that many struggle with due to sexual abuse. This is not to say that female victims hurt any less, but the way our society is set up, males feel the pressure to not cry, respond to pain or show any type of weakness.

When children are violated it is of the utmost importance that they are not ignored, blamed, or even scolded. The wrong response from an adult can easily cause a child to shut down emotionally and continue to suffer silently. Any child that has been abused needs to receive counseling and have a strong support system. Prayer coupled with counseling can help a child heal emotionally and move on to their bright future. A lack of prayer and counseling on the other hand can cause a hurting child to turn to drugs and alcohol as a means to cope or even fall into a perverted lifestyle. Many people without proper help carry these issues into other relationships and others might even become predators. Abuse has the ability to reposition the posture of our children's heart and skew their worldview and perspective of life. No matter what form of abuse is applicable it is important that the stings of abuse do not detour or even destroy the lives of our children.

The Budding Personality

<u>4</u>

According to the professional community, the personality is seen as the interaction of temperament traits with the child's environment. Temperament is considered to be innate traits that help a child organize his or her approach to the world.[1]

As believers, we know that as human beings we are a spirit in a body that possesses a soul. Our soul is inclusive of our mind, will, and emotions. We can therefore think of our personality as the expression of our soul. In other words, the way we think, behave and feel are all an expression of who we are as an individual. There are things about us that can be considered innate or a part of us from birth. For example, when you see a child with similar mannerisms, facial expressions and behaviors of a parent they have never met you can easily see the power of innate traits that we are born with.

As a child grows and develops our prayer is that our children develop a healthy and normal personality. By developing a healthy and normal personality a child will have a better

---

[1] Pappas, S. (2017, September 7). Personality Traits & Personality Types: What is Personality? New York, NY, USA.

perspective on life and have a better chance of developing healthy relationships, making good decisions, and living a successful and balanced life. When referring to a healthy and normal personality this is in contrast to an individual that could be diagnosed as having a personality disorder. Personality disorders are still considered rather difficult to treat as it relates to mental health disorders.

Some children will naturally have a happier and outgoing personality, while others are more withdrawn and quiet. There is nothing wrong with either because people are different and uniquely made by God. But there are some personality and character issues that have to be dealt with. There are a variety of reasons that a child's personality can be influenced negatively including trauma, neglect, depression, rejection, and addiction connected to their mother while they are still in the womb.

Children + Mental Health

As children begin to grow and develop their personality it is quintessential to watch for red flags. Sometimes parents think a child will grow out of negative behaviors and personality traits but this usually is not true. In a lot of situations that undesired quality will become deeply embedded and interwoven in them and if not caught early on could require extensive deliverance later on in life.

There are some red flags that are not as easily caught as others. A child that never has a desire to engage with other people might slip through the cracks while a child who kills animals and participates in acts of bestiality would stick out more. Watch out for personality flaws such as rage, violent temper, excessively withdrawn, lying, stealing and even crippling fear or anxiety. The enemy loves to destroy people in their formative years while they are yet children. He chips away at them little by little until he can gain full access. This is why we have to pray and instill the Word of God in our children. The enemy knows if he is able to cause our children to have an unhealthy personality by polluting and perverting their minds that he can hinder the plans of God.

As parents we have to make our child's mental health a priority. This means taking them to receive professional counseling and keeping them in counseling for as long as necessary. It is easy to look online and find a list of licensed professional Christian counselors in your area. Listed below are a few reasons you should consider getting counseling for your child(ren).

1. Child is a victim of abuse (sexual, physical, verbal etc.).
2. Parent(s) struggle with addiction to drugs and/or alcohol.
3. Absent parents or incarcerated parents
4. Child has been in the foster care system
5. Parental abandonment (given away at birth)
6. Witnessing violence or drug use.
7. Extreme poverty [home infested with rodents or bugs, no running water, no heat, living in condemned housing, food shortage]
8. Forced abortion or pregnancy via incest
9. Bullying and being shunned by peers
10. Adoption or not knowing the identity of one or both parents.

Guard Them

5

Children can be easily influenced by things that are good or evil. This means we must be careful of what we allow to have access to our children because many ungodly things can become planted and rooted in their hearts. As believers we guard our gates, but a 5-year-old child does not understand this concept so it is our job to monitor what they see, hear, handle or feel, taste or speak, and smell. Our 5 natural senses play a role into what is influencing our mind and could possibly get into our hearts.

Eye & Ear Gate

We must be selective as to what we allow our children to see and hear and this can refer to conversations, TV, music, video games, movies and things of that nature. Children are sponges and they absorb and adjust to their environment very easily. It confuses me how parents will use profanity in the presence of their children but then punish them for using the same words. If this scenario confuses me, I know it has to be painfully confusing to the children. It is understandable that our children will eventually hear profanity in our current society but it should not come from the lips of their parents.

Anything we allow our children to do for endless hours can become a powerful influence. We think that so many things are innocent when in actuality they are rooted in wickedness. How many parents have encouraged their children to read the most popular books on witches and warlocks but never the bible? And according to the Word of God we know that witchcraft is an abomination to the Lord. Witchcraft is the same as rebellion so to allow our children to read and watch materials that are about witchcraft is not a good idea as it could cause children to become curious or even pursue magic, potions, sorcery and things of that nature.

> **I Samuel 15:23**" For rebellion is as the sin of witchcraft, and stubbornness is as iniquity and idolatry. Because thou hast rejected the word of the LORD, he hath also rejected thee from being king." (KJV)

The eye gate is so powerful which is why Jesus talked about lusting after a woman by looking at her. Jesus was showing that what we see can get into our heart and cause us to sin against God. When our children are playing video games or watching and listening to anything that promotes violence, sex, drugs or any other demonic agenda this is a recipe for disaster. I am not naïve nor am I unrealistic to the fact that it is nearly impossible to shield our children from every negative influence but we can ensure that they are not constantly watching, hearing, and being surrounded by these things.

> **Matthew 5:28**" But I say unto you, that whosoever looketh on a woman to lust after her hath committed adultery with her already in his heart."(KJV)

The world of entertainment in the form of television and music are indoctrinating our children at an alarming rate. Unfortunately, this is causing them to rebel against the Word of God. In life all things cannot be avoided but they can be minimized by parents not allowing their children to be entertained by things focused on witchcraft and magic or listening to music that promotes perversion and rebellion. When you look at certain kid television channels almost every show is inclusive of witches, twitches, warlocks, psychics or some other form of witchcraft packaged as a show for children. Although these shows are popular and even highly entertaining what message is that sending our children and what subliminal messages are being impressed on their subconscious mind?

As parents we must be careful of allowing children to access the internet or cable television as they may inadvertently or even out of curiosity view pornography. It is a well-known fact that adults all over the world struggle with an addiction to pornography. We do not want our children exposed to the uncleanliness and perversion that pornography brings. This is an easy way for the enemy to plant demonic seeds and pollute our children's mind with perverted and filthy thoughts and cause them to engage in all sorts of sinful acts. Once a child has seen and heard too much it is hard to get them back to a place of innocence in the sense of not knowing things that are highly inappropriate for children. Eventually when children are a certain age and parents feel it is appropriate, they should teach their children about sex and reproduction. However, this lesson should not come from an X-rated film.

Psalm 101:3 "I will set no wicked thing before mine eyes: I hate the work of them that turn aside; it shall not cleave to me."

I hear children all the time singing and rapping sexually charged lyrics from their favorite celebrities but the same children cannot quote a scripture from the bible. It is time for Spirit-led parents to feed our children the Word of God and stop allowing the sphere of entertainment to indoctrinate our children to the ways of the world. We must serve our generation and raise up an army for the Kingdom of God.

Mouth Gate

What do we allow to come in and out of our mouths let alone the mouths of our children? All over social media there are videos of toddlers who are using profanity like professionals. These children are also smoking marijuana and doing cocaine. It is shameful, heartbreaking and infuriating to watch parents openly destroy their children by allowing them to use drugs and profanity at such a young age. What we allow our children to consume could one day consume them. There is no reason any Christian parent should allow their underage child to consume alcohol and smoke in their home with their reasoning being at least I know where they are when they are drinking. Not only is that illegal but that is absolutely preposterous to send that message to an underage child who is being raised in a self-proclaimed Christian home. When our children have a desire to engage in things that are not good for them, we should not aid them in their quests.

> **I Corinthians 6:19-20** "What? know ye not that your body is the temple of the Holy Ghost which is in you, which ye have of God, and ye are not your own? For ye are bought with a price: therefore, glorify God in your body, and in your spirit, which are God's." (KJV)

Hand & Nose Gate

Unlike the eyes, ears and mouth many times the hands and nose are negated but they also play a role as it relates to guarding your gates. How many times have you smelled or touched something and it triggered a memory or even altered your mood? This is why even the hands and nose also matter when it comes to guarding our gates.

There are certain smells and objects children should not be able to access regularly. Unless being trained to hunt and shoot by a responsible adult a child should not be allowed to handle guns and knives. Nor should they be allowed to handle drug paraphernalia or drugs including prescription drugs that do not belong to them. Smells of marijuana, crack cocaine, methamphetamine, alcohol or any other substance should not be arousing the senses of our children. Just the smell alone is powerful enough to lure in an unsuspecting child.

We should be teaching our children that their bodies are the temple of the Holy Spirit. And, that we should not pollute our bodies but rather yield them to God for His service. Our eyes should be used to read the Word and our ears to hear the Word. We should use our hands to pray for the sick and our mouths to praise God. We want our children to serve the Lord in the days of their youth (Ecclesiastes 12:1) and to praise Him with their whole heart in singing, shouting and dancing. Sometimes our expectations for our children are too low and we do not take the time to explain things and show them what God says in His word. Yes, children are not perfect and will have flaws in one area or another but we should not expect nor accept our children being sent off to prison or strung out on drugs as the will of God.

It is God's will for all to prosper and be in health even as our souls prosper (3 John 1:2). God's will can never oppose His written Word. So, when children do go astray their sins were not God's will but He is ready and able to turn our mess into a message or take our misery and make it a ministry. Because we live in a society where negative scenarios can unfold around our children on a daily basis, we have to explain these things and show them the pros and cons as well as what the Word says so they will not be caught off guard. Whatever is entering them through their gates along with their immediate influences and environment, come together to play a vital role in the development of our children.

D'Andrea M. Bolden

Footsteps to follow

<u>6</u>

Psalms 37:37" Mark the perfect man and behold the upright: for the end of that man is peace." (KJV)

As our children grow and develop they should not have to look any further to find guidance, a role model, or a good example. We teach our children about God by being a living example that they can see all the time. It is counterproductive to teach them the Word and do the opposite by teaching them to lie and be deceitful. We should not have our children lying for us or acting deceitfully for our benefit. We need to be examples in word and deed in and out of our homes.

It is counterproductive to send our children to church to learn about God and then they return home to a chaotic ungodly environment. There needs to be a similitude between our home and the message at our local assembly. In other words, our children should not learn about the fruit of the Spirit at church and come home to get cussed out and mistreated.

In general, children should learn about God at home more than at church. It is the job of parents to teach children about the Word and about God it should only be reinforced and strengthened at our local assembly. Many parents have the same attitude towards education and they will just send them out and feel they should learn all they need to know from their teachers. The greatest teachers in my children's lives are their father and mother.

Quality Time

It is sad when you see adults in ministry who have children but pour into others more than their own offspring. What good is it to evangelize the nations and lose your own household? We have to invest our time, money and resources into our children. Children most of often want our time and attention more than anything else. Even if the conversation is boring my daughter is excited because she is spending time with mom and dad. My son is much younger and only a toddler so the approach we have with him is different because he is in a distinct developmental stage. But we try to allot time to spend with both of our children. We try to make the best of the time we have with our growing children by taking advantage of teachable moments.

We have a short amount of time to prepare our children to survive and thrive in our current society. Spending too little time with our children can cause them to gravitate to the wrong people, places, or things. We can put the right things in them but many times when children begin to feel they are not getting enough attention they will begin to act out.

Mixed Signals

Mixed signals just indicate that a message; is not being clearly presented, is tainted, or that the lines are blurred. I know a lot of adults who no longer attend church because of their parents. They have watched their fathers preach on

Sunday and go home and beat on his wife. They have witnessed their parents living as swingers or having numerous adulterous affairs. Children are affected by their parent's actions when they are stealing, embezzling money, gambling, lying, cursing, fighting, using drugs or exhibiting any other type of morally corrupt behavior. Many young people have listened to way too many conversations where their parents talked about any and everybody in the church. We have to be living examples before our children day and night in word and deed. And although we all fall short and make mistakes when it affects our children sometimes, we need to apologize to them and get it right. If I get caught up in a drunken brawl in front of my children, I would feel convicted enough to repent to God and to apologize to my children for that behavior and explain that it is wrong. One thing about children they are always watching and listening even when we do not think that they are.

Growing in Grace

7

Growth is not something that happens without effort or automatically. Even flowers need water and light in order to continue growing. The same concept can be applied to our children because their gifts, talents, spiritual growth and personal development does not happen without effort and is not automatic.

I strongly believe that it is important to invest in our children by allowing them to attend conferences, take instructional classes, or get various opportunities to learn and grow. Allowing them to glean and learn from other people that have a greater level of expertise, knowledge and experience is a great way for them to grow and mature in their various gifts. Parents will send their children to football camp, basketball camp, track camp and even cheerleading camp but many overlook the importance of investing in their spiritual development. We always have to remember one plants, one waters but only God gives the increase (I Corinthians 3:6-9). This is not a job we can solely do on our own so when there are opportunities for our children to learn and grow or even receive impartation, we should embrace these opportunities. We do not want to be so overbearing and controlling that we never allow our children the chance to grow.

If your child is a psalmist or young minstrel there is nothing wrong with them taking lessons or learning from a more developed individual or even attending a seminar or conference. Having the mindset that your child can only function within your denomination or your church will slowly hinder them if not completely kill their gifting and their desire to use their gift. Being legalistic and overly religious is a common factor and reason that destiny and purpose is aborted by our children and why many of them walk away from church and never look back.

As parents we must use discretion and apply wisdom as to who we allow to have any influence in the lives of our children, but we must also not be close minded from a place of fear, suspicion, or self-righteousness. We must remain prayerful and watchful as our children engage with others because everyone does not have the right motives in their heart. Therefore, we must have our spiritual senses sharpened and in tune to be sure we are not allowing sheep to be amongst wolves that are cleverly disguised.

Identify Gifts & Talents

8

As fore stated, it is important to seek God to help us identity who He has created our children to be. Without the wisdom of God, a lot of parents try to force their children to fit a mold they have decided is appropriate. Many times, the child will become sad or even rebellious when they either fail miserably or have no pleasure in these things.

Once a child begins to walk and talk you will find that he or she will begin to slowly gravitate towards things that are of interest. You may see over time that a child has a love for dance, music, or even helping others. All these things seem minute when children are young but they can be indicators as to the gifts and talents that our children possess.

I will never forget one day in the summer of 2012 I was up very late (it was almost midnight). My daughter walked up to me with a look of sheer terror and panic on her face and she said that the devil was trying to destroy her and take something. I asked my daughter what was wrong and she said that she had had a bad dream but could not fully put in to words what happened so I prayed for her and also in her room and then she went back to sleep. The next day we sat down to discuss the dream and she told me that the devil was trying to destroy her and take her gifts and ability to sing and dance.

The enemy will do anything to either pervert or kill anything that God has placed in our children. I want my daughter to use her God given abilities to glorify God and not to allow those things to be perverted in the world.

One thing I did was take the time to teach my daughter about the fruit of the Spirit and the gifts of the Spirit. After I explained these things, I asked her what fruit she needed more of and what gifts she believed have been given to her by the Holy Spirit. On several occasions she was able to give a pretty good answer and also admitted the deficiencies in her character and behavior along with accurately identifying some of her spiritual gifts. Many times, if we take the time to teach children about gifts there are some they will naturally gravitate towards and many times those gifting are locked up on the inside of them. It is the duty of the parents to help our children identify their gifts and begin to learn and grow into these them along with their God ordained callings. We want to nurture their righteous desires and the things they show an interest in doing.

Recognizing Strengths and Weaknesses

Once a child reaches a certain age we should be able to see if they are truly excelling in something or if that might not be the best fit for them. Although there are great stories of blossoming into talents later in life such as Michael Jordan and basketball, this is not always the norm. We definitely want our children to find things they are passionate about and that they naturally excel in doing. This will help a child's confidence and self-esteem as they find their strengths and weaknesses. Even if a child is not the best at something if they love doing it, they should be encouraged to keep pursuing their desires. Children can be easily discouraged and de-motivated so we want to be cautious in how we approach them about certain matters. But it is pretty obvious when a child is miserable doing something and not very good at it. There is nothing wrong with recognizing that he or she just might flourish better in a different arena.

Some people love music but are awful singers. Yet, they may go on to become phenomenal song writers. A person might not have the best presence for dance but might be a better choreographer or instructor. Some children will be musicians and singers while others might do well at one or the other. Many young people are gifted poets, and some are exceptional spoken word performers. The point is that there is something for everyone and enough creativity for all. We must show them the options while recognizing both strengths and weaknesses. There are many adults who are struggling because they have an identity crisis and are trying to be something God never ordained for their life. These types of people were either told they were something that they are not or never aided in identifying their gifts and talents and ultimately their calling. We should be able to recognize if our children are very outgoing and a social butterfly or more quiet and reserved. Is your child a natural born leader who is very organized and likes to bring forth order and structure? Children who find things that they are good at and enjoy doing are less likely to fall into deviant behavior.

Emphasizing Character Over Ability

It is important to ensure that our children's level of character matches their level of grace in their gifting. We have to desire that our children understand the importance of integrity (doing the right thing when no one is looking) and having righteous and Godly character. Nothing saddens me more than people who are blatantly sinning but they are still allowed to sing, dance, play instruments and even "preach" because they are gifted and talented.

One day, I asked my daughter if she would ever consider eating her dinner out of a garbage can and her reply, much like anyone else was a resounding no. I explained to her that she needs to give God her best and be a vessel of honor unto the Lord.

> **II Timothy 2:20-22**" But in a great house there are not only vessels of gold and of silver, but also of wood and of earth; and some to honour, and some to dishonour. If a man therefore purge himself from these, he shall be a vessel unto honour, sanctified, and meet for the master's use, and prepared unto every good work. Flee also youthful lusts: but follow righteousness, faith, charity, peace, with them that call on the Lord out of a pure heart." (KJV)

We have to emphasize and reiterate to our children that it is not enough to just be gifted but that their life needs to line up with what they are proclaiming in front of God's people. Many of today's preachers who started out as children and are now known for having a lack of character and being morally corrupt. However, on so many occasions they were given a pass simply because they are gifted.

When we see major character flaws such as greed, pride, lust, perversion, anger, rage or anything else operating in our children we should not allow them to keep using their gifts and talents in the house of the Lord without correction. They will need to come to a place of repentance and realizing the error of their ways. We do not want to raise another generation of people who are having "church" but do not know God. We have a mandate to teach the youth the way of the Lord and that which is right. Parents have allowed their children to become hirelings instead of consecrated minstrels, and singers instead of anointed psalmists.

I was in worship and the Lord showed me an opening in the heavens and a seemingly endless pile of gifts that have never been touched or utilized in anyway. That lets me know there is no lack in gifting from God but there is a lack of proper discipline and building godly character in our children. We have to come to a place where character is more important than allowing them to use their talents and gifts. I do not want to see anyone sit in church their whole life and use their gifts while walking in error and in the end miss heaven and their soul is lost forever.

God Speaks to Children

9

Joel 2:28" And it shall come to pass afterward, *that* I will pour out my spirit upon all flesh; and your sons and your daughters shall prophesy, your old men shall dream dreams, your young men shall see visions:" (KJV)

My daughter is a dreamer and God speaks to her clearly in dreams. Dreams are one of the many ways that God can speak to us for the purpose of conveying a certain message or truth to us. There are many examples in the bible that show how God spoke to His servants, kings and everyday men through a dream to reveal a truth. I remember one time my daughter told me she had a dream that she was in heaven with Jesus praying for people to be healed when she looked and saw my mother in law walking around on two legs. The reason this was so powerful is because my mother-in-law passed away a few years' prior and was a double amputee. I noticed that many of my daughter's dreams were about people being sick or having surgery and needing prayer and so I began to tell her to pray about what God shows her and to pray for those people.

I can still remember when my daughter was around 3 years old and she ran up to me and was trying to prophesy. She kept saying "God said" but nothing ever followed. This intrigued me and made me strongly desire for her to learn to hear the voice of the Lord for herself. I began spending Saturday mornings not only combing her hair but talking to her about the things of God and it is funny how children understand more than we believe they do. I would take the time to speak over her life and pray for her and I would ask her what God was saying to her and she would share what she felt God was saying and quite a few times she hit the nail on the head.

The Holy Spirit began to deal with my daughter a lot and I could tell when the Lord was whispering something in her ear. When the Holy Spirit would speak, she would be very still and have this look on her face. Later on, I would always ask her to share what the Lord had shared with her. I remember the first time she "heard" the voice of the Holy Spirit and I asked her how she knew and she responded, "because He spoke to my mind". She later began to ask about speaking in tongues and I took the time to teach her about the Holy Spirit and share the scriptures that discussed the Holy Spirit. She prayed to receive the Holy Spirit but did not speak in other tongues because she did not understand. I told her you cannot try and figure it out but I could tell she was highly disappointed and let down so I prayed and asked for the Lord to deal with her in a way she could understand. She got up the next morning and said she saw herself at the age of 38 years old and she was speaking in tongues before a crowd of people and that the power of God hit and everyone in the room was stretched out before the Lord. That reassured her that it would happen and gave her much joy. Shortly after that day she was sitting by herself and began to speak in tongues as the Holy Spirit gave utterance. God wants to release His love to our children and to comfort them in every way possible. He even desires to reveal things to come and show them His plans in a way they can understand.

My daughter Anaya has always been a gifted child and just like God would speak to her in dreams the enemy would come with nightmares. So many nights she would be harassed with nightmares of witches, and ghosts. My first reaction was to make sure she was not watching anything that was about ghosts, witches, goblins and things of that nature. Second, I made sure she did not have any witch or ghost's toys or books in the house. Then I began to teach her to plead the blood of Jesus and pray to God. Many nights both my husband and I would pray for her and in her room, but we knew she still needed to learn how to pray to God for herself. The enemy tried to place so much fear in her that she was afraid of the dark and I said no to that. I would make her walk through the house with me praying in the dark to show her there was no reason to be afraid.

It hurts me to my core when parents allow the enemy to torment their child with nightmares and they either do nothing or assume they will grow out of it. The assignment is to drive fear into the heart of the child, and they will not grow out of that in fact it will more than likely get stronger and harder to break over time. God desires not only to speak to children but also to use them. They are not too young if He can use a donkey, He can use a child. Children get excited when they realize God can and will use them. We must teach our children to learn to Hear the voice of the Lord for themselves. We do this by taking the time in prayer to see what the Lord is saying, and by instructing them on how to hear His voice. We have to teach our children the ways that God can speak to us by showing them in the Word of God.

D'Andrea M. Bolden

Identifying + Breaking Generational Curses

10

A curse is God's recompense in the life of a person and his or her descendants as a result of iniquity (Lamentations 3:65). Curses open the door for evil spirits and allow them legal grounds to purposely establish and perpetuate their wicked schemes and intentions in the lives of people. Discernment is necessary and key when being able to understand what possibly can be operating in the lives of our children. But we can also detect these generational curses by knowing our family history and patterns.

> **Deuteronomy 6:6-10**" And these words, which I command thee this day, shall be in thine heart: And thou shalt teach them diligently unto thy children, and shalt talk of them when thou sittest in thine house, and when thou walkest by the way, and when thou liest down, and when thou risest up. And thou shalt bind them for a sign upon thine hand, and they shall be as frontlets between thine eyes. And thou shalt write them upon the posts of thy house, and on thy gates. And it shall be, when the LORD thy God shall have brought thee into the land which he sware unto thy fathers, to Abraham, to Isaac, and to Jacob, to give thee great and goodly cities, which thou buildedst not," (KJV)

Two simple reasons why generational curses continue on is because of ignorance and undisclosed truths. Ignorance is a big issue because many people know little to nothing about their family lineage especially when they are adopted or abandoned by one or both parents. It is important that we let our children know about their family history including wickedness and iniquity that has traveled from generation to generation. The bible declares my people perish for a lack of knowledge. You cannot avoid a speeding train if no one tells you that it is coming. Children need to know the truth even if they only know the issues that plagued their parents.

Undisclosed truths on the other hand is when family secrets are purposely hidden either to avoid tarnish to the family name or due to embarrassment and shame. Hiding the truth from our children is a major reason generational curses are able to destroy families easily because no one will speak the truth so that the curse can be broken and stopped in the bloodline. Many of the things hidden from children usually deal with incest, rape, molestation and truths behind maternal and paternal identities to children. Sadly, hiding things does nothing but allow iniquitous patterns to grow stronger each and every generation. If we do not take the time to tell our children the truth about things that have occurred in the lives of their ancestors, we allow them to be blindsided and many times walk into the same situation unaware.

Whether ignorance or undisclosed truths generational curses love to continue on unchallenged from one generation to the next. In the bible let's take a look at Isaac and Abram both he and his father were in the exact same situation and made the exact same decision. I highly doubt that he rehearsed and prepared for the day he would fall prey to the same situation that occurred to his father years prior but look at what happened.

Abram and Sarai

> **Genesis 12:10-20" And there was a famine in the land: and Abram went down into Egypt to sojourn there**; for the famine was grievous in the land. ¹¹And it came to pass, when he was come near to enter into Egypt, that he said unto Sarai his wife, **Behold now, I know that thou art a fair woman to look upon: ¹²Therefore it shall come to pass, when the Egyptians shall see thee, that they shall say, This is his wife: and they will kill me, but they will save thee alive. ¹³Say, I pray thee, thou art my sister: that it may be well with me for thy sake; and my soul shall live because of thee.** ¹⁴And it came to pass, that, when Abram was come into Egypt, the Egyptians beheld the woman that she was very fair. ¹⁵The princes also of Pharaoh saw her, and commended her before Pharaoh: and the woman was taken into Pharaoh's house. ¹⁶And he entreated Abram well for her sake: and he had sheep, and oxen, and he asses, and menservants, and maidservants, and she asses, and camels. ¹⁷And the LORD plagued Pharaoh and his house with great plagues because of Sarai Abram's wife. **¹⁸And Pharaoh called Abram, and said, What is this that thou hast done unto me? why didst thou not tell me that she was thy wife? ¹⁹Why saidst thou, She is my sister? so I might have taken her to me to wife: now therefore**

behold thy wife, take her, and go thy way. ²⁰And Pharaoh commanded his men concerning him: and they sent him away, and his wife, and all that he had" (KJV)

Isaac and Rebekah

Genesis 26:1-11" And there was a famine in the land, beside the first famine that was in the days of Abraham. And Isaac went unto Abimelech king of the Philistines unto Gerar. ²And the LORD appeared unto him, and said, Go not down into Egypt; dwell in the land which I shall tell thee of: ³Sojourn in this land, and I will be with thee, and will bless thee; for unto thee, and unto thy seed, I will give all these countries, and I will perform the oath which I sware unto Abraham thy father; ⁴And I will make thy seed to multiply as the stars of heaven, and will give unto thy seed all these countries; and in thy seed shall all the nations of the earth be blessed; ⁵Because that Abraham obeyed my voice, and kept my charge, my commandments, my statutes, and my laws. ⁶And Isaac dwelt in Gerar: ⁷**And the men of the place asked him of his wife; and he said, She is my sister: for he feared to say, She is my wife; lest, said he, the men of the place should kill me for Rebekah; because she was fair to look upon.** ⁸And it came to pass, when he had been there a long time, that Abimelech king of the Philistines looked out at a window, and saw, and, behold, Isaac was sporting with Rebekah his wife. ⁹**And Abimelech called Isaac, and said, Behold, of a surety she is thy wife: and how saidst thou, She is my sister? And Isaac said unto him, Because I said, Lest I die for her.** ¹⁰And Abimelech said, What is this thou hast done unto us? one of the people might lightly have lien with thy wife, and thou shouldest have brought guiltiness upon us. ¹¹And Abimelech charged all his people, saying, He that toucheth this man or his wife shall surely be put to death." (KJV)

After reading the scriptures we can see that Isaac made the same decision in the same situation as his father did many years prior. How many times have you witnessed the grandfather, father and son all in prison at the same time for nearly the same identical crime? What about when every woman in the family ends up an alcoholic? These are not just mere coincidences these are the symptoms of unchallenged generational curses.

Look at King David he defeated many giants but he never killed the giant of lust in his life and we can see how it overtook his son and how his heart was eventually turned away from God. When parents struggle with lust and perversion, they must let their children know regardless of how embarrassing it might be to them. If a parent participated in acts of bestiality, molestation, homosexuality or even incest they need to let their children know so that they will not unknowingly engage in the same iniquitous behavior as his or her ancestors.

> **I Kings 11:1-6**" But king Solomon loved many strange women, together with the daughter of Pharaoh, women of the Moabites, Ammonites, Edomites, Zidonians, and Hittites: ² Of the nations concerning which the LORD said unto the children of Israel, Ye shall not go in to them, neither shall they

come in unto you: for surely they will turn away your heart after their gods: Solomon clave unto these in love.³ And he had seven hundred wives, princesses, and three hundred concubines: and his wives turned away his heart.⁴ For it came to pass, when Solomon was old, that his wives turned away his heart after other gods: and his heart was not perfect with the LORD his God, as was the heart of David his father.⁵ For Solomon went after Ashtoreth the goddess of the Zidonians, and after Milcom the abomination of the Ammonites.⁶ And Solomon did evil in the sight of the LORD, and went not fully after the LORD, as did David his father." (KJV)

Curses that are visible

In most cases we cannot see a generational curse with our naked eye but we can identify it through our spiritual eyes. A person can be walking down the street but you cannot see a generational curse of infertility. One-way generational curses can become "visible" to the naked eye is through expressed genetic material or being made manifest in our physical body. As a human being we have 23 pairs of chromosomes in the nucleus of each somatic cell. The 23rd pair identifies the gender with either XX chromosomes for a female or XY for a male. On the chromosomes are genes and they are the basic physical and functional unit of heredity. A gene can be considered an informational storage unit that has the ability to be expressed, replicated or mutated. Within our DNA many times there are variations of the same gene called alleles. As a simplistic understandable example tall (T) and dwarf (t) are alleles that can determine the height of an individual.

Many times, family members carry similar genetic material especially those that are closely related such as immediate family members. When family members began to intermix, any child produced has a chance of getting some similar genetic material from the two parents. I know that incest is a very taboo topic and many do not want to speak on it but incest is a vehicle the enemy has and is still using to infiltrate the bloodlines of many families. When incest is allowed to run rampant in a family and offspring are produced that is how genetic issues can come easily into play. This is why people would say you cannot date your relatives or your child would have 3 hands or 5 eyes and things like this. They were not exactly correct yet they were actually on to something.

Many individuals within families are carriers of rare and undesirable diseases and ailments but that genetic information is not *expressed* so they are to be considered normal and healthy. But when individuals from that same family begin to reproduce via close incestuous relationships their children can be born with these rare conditions and issues. When two relatives that are carriers for the same genetic material reproduce their child can get that same undesirable DNA from each parent.

There was a family a few years back that denied incest but they all lived isolated and had an extremely rare disorder that caused them to literally be the color blue. This is a prime example of what generations of incestuous relationships can do especially when you see disorders that should be rare become common within a family. Incest has the ability to manifest in the physical body through reproduction.

Although issues such as incest are hard for many people to admit it is imperative that our children know the truth. Many people in the have hidden the truth only to be crushed by their sons and daughters having relationships with each other. Incestuous relationships are more common than many people are aware of because it remains hidden a lot. Whether incest in one's family is consensual or by force (rape) hiding this only allows it to continue on from one generation to the next. It is sad to see generations of broken children grow into adults who struggle with addiction and a plethora of other issues that are all rooted in incest.

Break The Curse

According to Galatians 3:13 we are redeemed from the curse and because of the work of Jesus Christ we are able to receive God's love, forgiveness, and deliverance.

> **Galatians 3:13**" Christ hath redeemed us from the curse of the law, being made a curse for us: for it is written, Cursed is everyone that hangeth on a tree:" (KJV)

When we identify curses that need to be broken, we first renounce these things and repent and then we break these curses in the name of Jesus and we command all spirits that have entered and operated through that curse to come out of his or her life in Jesus' name.

Parents have the authority and the duty as the spiritual authority and head of their children to identify and shut every door that the enemy has or can use to gain entry to their lives.

Balancing It Out

11

It is important that children have a balance between natural and spiritual things. It would be irrational to feel that children should be forced to fast and pray day and night. There still needs to be room for the run and play and enjoyment of being a kid. As adults we should exercise wisdom by not being overbearing and causing our children to despise church and the things of God. We should never overwhelm them with perfectionism or trying to be a "blameless" child.

They should still be able to enjoy their childhood and play sports and have hobbies. Some parents unintentionally overlook the opportunity to disciple their children and teach them about God. On the other hand, some parents want children to display the same level of maturity as a 75-year-old pastor which is unrealistic. When children are learning we should teach them in a strategic manner. In school children learn things that are appropriate to their level of understanding which is why it would be silly for someone to attempt to teach a child about spiritual warfare but never take the time to teach them about the testimony of Jesus Christ.

Well Rounded

As believers we want to raise children that are well-rounded and able to flourish in our current society. This is why we not only want our children to be disciples of the Word but also prepared to function as productive citizens. We bring a balance to their Christian upbringing with an adequate education, sharpening their talents and skills and giving them life skills that will be applicable to them as they transition into adulthood. We want to be practical to make sure our children have common sense on top of their faith-based foundation. I have found some parents have raised their children to be doomsday prepared or so heavenly minded that they are no earthly good. We do not want our children raised in a state of fear waiting for pending doom because we know the future is in God's hands.

Instead of raising our children to prepare for absolute chaos and doom we should prepare them to be both salt and light in the earth that they might wins souls for the Kingdom of God. Our children are ambassadors for Christ everywhere they go and they have the ability to let the light of Christ shine through them. This is why we need our children in every sphere that is governing our society such as politics, science, entertainment, education, economics and so forth. They will function in these various spheres not to be conformed but to shift the agenda by standing on the principles found in the Word of God.

Everyone's assignment is different and some of our children may do great exploits for the Kingdom in corporate America and never the pulpit. Some of our children may be called to the marketplace and some may travel the world for foreign missions. Regardless of their God ordained destiny and path they choose we want them to be balanced and well-rounded that they can flourish in any setting.

Children need a balance so that they are able to comfortably interact and function in society.

D'Andrea M. Bolden

Prophetic Stirring

12

God desires to deal with children while they are young but sadly this doesn't always happen. God wants to stir up the gifting that is on the inside of our children. But they are unable to do this without our help to teach them and point them in the right direction.

Recognizing the voice of the Lord

> **I Samuel 3:1-9** "And the child Samuel ministered unto the LORD before Eli. And the word of the LORD was precious in those days; there was no open vision. And it came to pass at that time, when Eli was laid down in his place, and his eyes began to wax dim, that he could not see; And ere the lamp of God went out in the temple of the LORD, where the ark of God was, and Samuel was laid down to sleep; That the LORD called Samuel: and he answered, Here am I. And he ran unto Eli, and said, Here am I; for thou calledst me. And he said, I called not; lie down again. And he went and lay down. And the LORD called yet again, Samuel. And Samuel arose and went to Eli, and said, Here am I; for thou didst call me. And he answered, I called not, my son; lie down again. Now Samuel did not yet know the LORD, neither was the word of the LORD yet revealed unto him. And the LORD called Samuel again the third time. And he arose and went to Eli, and said, Here am I; for thou didst call me. And Eli perceived that the LORD had

called the child. Therefore, Eli said unto Samuel, Go, lie down: and it shall be, if he call thee, that thou shalt say, Speak, LORD; for thy servant heareth. So Samuel went and lay down in his place." (KJV)

I find that God loves to begin to awaken prophetically gifted children while they are still young. Samuel is the perfect example of God awakening a prophetic gift at an early age. As you read through the passage you can see that God began to call Samuel by name but he thought it was Eli because he did not yet know the Lord as the scripture states. Eventually Eli perceives that the Lord is calling Samuel. Children have to learn the voice of the Lord but many times as parents we have to nudge them in the right direction. God began to deal with my daughter in dreams when she was very small so I had to begin to explain to her how important those dreams are and that God is speaking to her to reveal a message. God would show her people being sick with cancer, marital issues, or a move of God that was coming to our local assembly. In the process of God dealing with a prophetically gifted child the first thing they must recognize is the voice of the Lord.

Responding to God's Voice

I Samuel 3:9-10 " Therefore Eli said unto Samuel, Go, lie down: and it shall be, if he call thee, that thou shalt say, Speak, LORD; for thy servant heareth. So Samuel went and lay down in his place. And the LORD came, and stood, and called as at other times, Samuel, Samuel. Then Samuel answered, Speak; for thy servant heareth." (KJV)

After Eli realized that Samuel was hearing the voice of the Lord, he told Samuel how to respond. Hearing God's voice is one thing but responding is another. The scripture showed how Samuel responded when he heard God's voice again. It is a pretty simple concept if you are talking to someone and they never respond eventually you just stop talking and this holds true with our Heavenly Father. If God is speaking to us continuously and we never listen or respond eventually He will become silent until we are ready and willing to listen to His voice.

Acting on His Command

> **I Samuel 3:11-18** "And the LORD said to Samuel, Behold, I will do a thing in Israel, at which both the ears of every one that heareth it shall tingle. In that day I will perform against Eli all things which I have spoken concerning his house: when I begin, I will also make an end. For I have told him that I will judge his house for ever for the iniquity which he knoweth; because his sons made themselves vile, and he restrained them not. And therefore I have sworn unto the house of Eli, that the iniquity of Eli's house shall not be purged with sacrifice nor offering forever. And Samuel lay until the morning, and opened the doors of the house of the LORD. And Samuel feared to shew Eli the vision. Then Eli called Samuel, and said, Samuel, my son. And he answered, Here am I. And he said, What is the thing that the LORD hath said unto thee? I pray thee hide it not from me: God do so to thee, and more also, if thou hide anything from me of all the things that he said unto thee. And Samuel told him every whit, and hid

nothing from him. And he said, It is the LORD: let him do what seemeth him good" (KJV)

Once Samuel learned to recognize the voice of the Lord and was able to respond he then had to act on God's command. In other words, Samuel would have to do or say what God required of him. This passage shows that children are just as capable as adults if they are in the right environment to flourish. I am a firm believer that if children can be influenced by the enemy they can be used by the Lord to the fullest. Sometimes our expectations as parents can be lower than their level of potential. All children will grow into their prophetic abilities at different stages and rates according to their assignment, God's time of preparation for them and their cooperation with the Holy Spirit. Some children will be like Samuel and be called into ministry as a child while others will be called later in life at various stages.

Submitting to the process

> **I Samuel 3:19** "And Samuel grew, and the LORD was with him, and did let none of his words fall to the ground."

Children must submit to the processing of the Lord. It breaks my heart to see the rise and fall of young gifted vessels because they were not submitted to the process. Releasing a child into ministry full time or at any level without allowing them years of processing in order to develop character and integrity can be detrimental to their destiny.

No matter how gifted and anointed your child is you must resist releasing them before their time. Many due to accolades of man quickly are caught up in pride and develop a non-teachable spirit. They must continue to learn and grow it is not a coincidence that even Jesus Christ waited until the age of 30 before starting His ministry. Although everyone will not be 30 when they step into their calling it is imperative to realize the importance of being fully equipped and developed. Far too many young prophetic gifts have ended up corrupt, money hungry, liars, fornicators, drunkards, false prophets, and master manipulators. It is imperative that no matter how God begins to use our children that they understand they are not above leadership, correction, rebuke, or discipline. They also must know that God's processing takes time and that patience is needed to ensure they do not forego God's processing in order to step into ministry out of season.

Dealing With Rejection & Fear

> **1 Peter 2:4** "As you come to him, a living stone rejected by men but in the sight of God chosen and precious," (ESV)

Rejection and fear are two significant ways that the enemy loves to gain a foothold in order to hinder God's children. Rejection will cause a person to feel that they do not belong or fit. Rejected people may also feel a sense of being unloved, unwanted or even that they are a burden. Rejection can cause an individual to isolate themselves or to avoid people in order to avoid the pain of rejection. Children for many reasons may experience various forms of rejection. They can be rejected by parents or other family members, peers or even the opposite sex. I try to continuously remind

Prophetically Gifted Children

<u>13</u>

Prophetically gifted children are some of the most unique individuals but due to a lack of understanding they are easily mislabeled as crazy, weird or even strange. These children many times experience frequent supernatural encounters, dreams and visions. These supernaturally gifted children have the ability to excel in the seven spheres of the earth. This is why it is important to understand the personality, gifts, anointing and destiny of our children. As parents we have to recognize who they are and where they belong in order to help prepare them both naturally and spiritually during their formative years.

For example, if a young child excels greatly in math and science they could possibly be called to work in the medical field or even in academia but either way spirit filled believers are greatly needed in both areas. Understanding these things ahead of time helps us to prepare them naturally to have a plan and path for their future vocation. There are some doors that will not be opened without the proper education no matter how great the spiritual gifting and anointing is on your child. Your child could hold the key to extraordinary medical breakthroughs in cancer research but if they never get the proper education they will not be allowed to work and function in that capacity and the world will never know or benefit from the greatness that God placed on the inside of them.

We cannot negate the importance of understanding how the natural and spiritual coincide as it relates to the assignment God places in these unique individuals. To think that the sole purpose God places prophetically gifted children in the earth is limited to prophesy is absolutely preposterous.

God is adamant on getting a hold of these unique children early in life but so is the kingdom of darkness. For this reason alone, parents have to be aware of the encounters their child might be having. Many of the prophets I know have stated that as children they were visited by demonic spirits disguised as a deceased loved one. This a tactic the enemy uses to get a hold of their spiritual "antennas" to keep them occupied and to lead them astray so that they will be unable to become tuned in to the voice of the Lord. The reason knowing the voice of the Lord is so important is because as divine communicators they must be able to clearly hear His instructions. Nothing about prophetically gifted children is a mistake or an accident as you can read in Psalm 139:13-18. As His Creation, God perfected them even in the womb. All of the intricate details of your child's life are written in His book. They were made in secret for a specific purpose that must be made manifest in the earth.

> **Psalms 139:13-18** "For You did form my inward parts; You did knit me together in my mother's womb. I will confess *and* praise You *for You are fearful and wonderful and* for the awful wonder of my birth! Wonderful are Your works, and that my inner self knows right well. My frame was not hidden from You when I was being formed in secret [and] intricately *and* curiously wrought [as if

embroidered with various colors] in the depths of the earth [a region of darkness and mystery]. Your eyes saw my unformed substance, and in Your book all the days [of my life] were written before ever they took shape, when as yet there was none of them. How precious *and* weighty also are Your thoughts to me, O God! How vast is the sum of them! If I could count them, they would be more in number than the sand. When I awoke, [could I count to the end] I would still be with You" (Amplified   version)

The nature of prophetically gifted children

Prophetically gifted children have a high tendency to be extremely visual and very innovative by nature. This is why some of the most profound inventions, songs, medical breakthroughs, technological concepts and ingenious ideas have been revealed to prophetically gifted people through dreams and visions. Most of the time these people do not realize the scope, nature and source of their gifts and talents but that can change by us preparing and teaching our prophetically gifted children who they really are in God. Because of their ability to flourish beyond the average person it should be no shock that many of the world's greatest singers, songwriters, playwrights, authors, musicians, dancers and artists are prophetically gifted people.

It is our job as parents to ensure our children not only recognize their gifts and talents but also how they should properly be used. What should have been the greatest psalmists, minstrels, praise dancers and musical geniuses have utilized their gifts and talents in the world for many reasons. One of the greatest reasons is not being raised in an environment that would help them understand or flourish in their gifts. Many times, a lot of parents are clueless as to the purpose and depth of the gifts and talents possessed by their children. Another common reason is not having any opportunities to use their gift in the church due to the rigors of religion and the traditions of man. And lastly many have also felt that the church did not and would not honor or value their gift like the secular arena. The greatest thing we can do is teach our children the importance of worship and show them the heart of worship before emphasizing that they perfect their gifts and talents. This will shift the posture of a lot of hearts. Without a true biblical understanding of worship people cannot comprehend the difference between a singer and psalmist, musician and minstrel, or dancer and worshipping dancer. When people feel that worship is the equivalence of 2 fast songs and 2 slows songs, they have a great need to be taught the biblical model for pure worship unto the Lord.

There are some other common areas where prophetically gifted children stand out. Later in life they usually make great counselors, lawyers and even police officers. The wisdom, discernment and insight of prophetically gifted people allow them to flourish in these types of careers.

When we look at prophetically gifted children, they are flat out different to say the least and they must learn to embrace their difference. They will see and hear things differently from those around them. They will many times feel like a round hole and square peg in many cases. Fitting in a lot of times will not always be an option as they will many times be misunderstood for no apparent reason.

Avoiding pitfalls

Prophetically gifted children are naturally drawn to the supernatural, but this can sometimes get them ensnared by powers of darkness. In many scenarios a lot of churches are not operating in the supernatural power of God and this leaves no genuine outlet for these prophetically gifted people in the church. Therefore, many of them inadvertently fall into occult practices in order to feed their natural cravings for supernatural power, manifestations and phenomena. There are many people who are truly called to be prophets but instead they are operating as psychics because in many cases they do not realize what they are doing is wrong and that the source of their information is demonic. We have to ensure there are safe and structured outlets in the house of the Lord for our children to grow and be trained in their gifts. I train children in the prophetic in a similar to the way that I handle adults and this is imperative so they can begin to understand the dreams they are having and begin to filter the "voices" and truly learn to discern the voice of the Lord. Proper teaching and training during their formative years can allow them to avoid many demonic pitfalls down the road.

Ultimately prophetically gifted children have been entrusted by God to fulfill a great purpose that requires them to be wired a bit different when compared to everyone else. They are to live a life of obedience and servitude before the Lord.

The gifts, resources and abilities allotted to them is not for their own gain but for God to be glorified in the earth. Their purpose and their assignment are tailor made to fit their abilities, personality and intellect.

Deliverance & Children

14

In order to avoid seeing the full manifestation of the workings of demonic spirits in the lives of our children we must realize they need deliverance too. To deny our children the ministry of deliverance is to allow their inner-man to be polluted and tainted in one way or another. Most will agree that the majority of the bondage in a person's life can be traced back to their childhood. Parents that ignore and neglect the development of their child's personality [which is the function and expression of their soul] is a tragic mistake. Neglecting the spiritual aspect of parenting is allowing demonic spirits the ability to enjoy an open season and a feasting on our children. Handling parenting from a completely natural approach can allow our children to grow up with constant thoughts of unnatural desires, identity issues, along with other root issues that can lead them to destruction. Root issues refers to strongholds such as parental abandonment, fear, abuse, neglect, rejection and so forth.

Root issues must be dealt with in order to have a healthy heart, thought life, desires and emotions. Issues have a way of skewing our perspective and can block us from having the correct approach in both our natural and spiritual lives. The unique experiences that our children will encounter and experience in life are able to taint their souls and the lens by which they view life. Rape, domestic violence, abandonment and even rejection are all able to have a negative impact in the souls of our children.

Deliverance early on can hinder the strengthening of strongholds, cancel demonic assignments and break generational curses. A healthy soul will allow our children to be well-balanced individuals. Parents that understand deliverance are able to quickly identify and combat against demonic spirits trying to gain full access to operate in their child's life. Demonic spirits will try and gain access to our children through the bloodline, the womb, trauma, abuse and so forth. This is why we have children younger and younger making demonic declarations over their lives.

Below is a list of common areas where our children tend to need ministry and prayer.

Fear

Nightmares and Night terrors: A lot of children are harassed late at night by nightmares and demonic encounters. This can be an avenue for the spirit of fear to gain access to their lives.

False Burdens: A lot of children are taking on the burdens of their parents and are even in a panic about life itself falling apart because they have taken on burdens that do not belong to them.

Trauma: Traumatic experiences have the ability to leave a strong impression on the soul of a person. For many people this can mean the fear of the traumatic event happening again.

Occultic Practices & Demonic Entertainment: Demonic entertainment is an easy way for the enemy to gain access to the lives of our children. This can cause constant torment and harassment from demonic spirits.

Ouija boards, tarot cards, horror movies, crystal balls, psychics, mediums, séances, books on the occult, toys that portray demonic spirits and deities.

Abuse

Abuse comes in many shapes and forms but any type of abuse has the ability to skew the way a person views life, themselves or even God. The pain of abuse is powerful enough to hold a person captive their entire life. Abuse and trauma can reshape a person's personality in a negative way.

Types of abuse:

1. Physical

2. Verbal

3. Sexual

4. Emotional

Abandonment

Abandonment is hard on anyone but it can be especially hard on children. Abandonment works in conjunction with rejection, fear, and bitterness. Abandonment is an easy way for the enemy to gain access to the soul of person. The void left causes insecurities along with difficulties and abnormalities as it relates to relationships.

1. Abandonment & rejection by parents

2. Parental neglect and delinquency

3. Abandonment by parents and family (at birth or in childhood)

Poverty

Poverty is their destruction (Prov 10:15). Poverty affects the way people view life and the decisions they make. Poverty works hand in hand with destructive thinking and lifestyles. If you take the time to visit any neighborhood that is filled with poverty you will find violence, lawlessness, rebellion, ignorance, abuse, addiction and any other destructive and sinful practices one can name. Poverty is able to crush a person's hopes and dreams. Many young children raised in poverty give up on any hope that they can ever overcome the crushing blow of poverty.

Rebellion

Rebellion causes one to always go against the grain so to speak. Rebellion will allow an individual to constantly be disobedient to all authority including God and His Word. Rebellion will cause people to even rebel against boundaries that keep them safe. Rebellion will cause a child to completely disconnect from the voice and authority of their parents in order to express their own will.

1. Rebellion against authority

2. Rebellion against parents

3. Rebellion against God's word and the Truth of His Word

4. Rebellion against rules and societal norms

Rejection

Rejection is major issue because everyone has experienced rejection. Even our children have to deal with rejection.

1. Rejection from Peers

2. Rejection from the Opposite Sex

3. Rejection from the womb

> Gender Rejection. (stronger if parents continue to reiterate, they wanted the opposite gender and this can ultimately open the door to sexual immorality and confusion). Also, relevant if one or both of the parents contemplated and considered abortion of the child

4. Feeling Unloved/Unwanted

5. Rejection from parents and family

Generational Curses

Identify all generational curses that are applicable to both sides of the family. It is important to recognize what is in the bloodline from both the mother and father. Generational curses will continue on within your family bloodline until challenged. We are to renounce and cast these spirits out of the bloodline in Jesus' name.

Examples of Generational Curses

1. Addiction
2. Poverty
3. Perversion
4. Mental Illness
5. Sickness & Infirmity
6. Incest
7. Witchcraft
8. Short Life

Prayers, Declarations and Decrees

15

Decree: An official order issued by a legal authority

Declaration: A formal or explicit statement or announcement

Prayer: Is our formal communication with God.

Below are declaration, decrees, scriptures and prayers to release and speak over certain areas of our children's lives.

FEAR

Common areas: Fear of the dark, fear of death, fear of rejection, fear of failure, fear of demons, nightmares and night terrors, fear caused by traumatic events, fear of being alone

I declare that fear has no place in my child's life.

I decree that all assignments of fear against my son/daughter's life is broken in Jesus name

> **II Timothy 1:7**" For God has not given us a spirit of fear, but of power and of love and of a sound mind."

I John 4:18 "There is no fear in love; but perfect love casteth out fear: because fear hath torment. He that feareth is not made perfect in love."

Heavenly Father, according to Your Word, You have not given me a spirit of fear, but instead You have given me a spirit of power of love and of a sound mind. Lord, I thank you for removing all forms of fear and torment from my child's life. Lord, in your Word You said, that Your love casts out all fear. Father I thank you now for Your love going into the depths of my child's mind, will and emotions. In Jesus' name Amen.

PERVERSION

Common areas: sexual perversion, twisted/unnatural desires, perverted use and abuse of physical body, perverted relationship with other children or adults,

I declare that perversion has no dominion in my child's life.

I decree that every demonic attack and tactic of the enemy against my child's life that is rooted and connected to the spirit of perversion is canceled and destroyed in Jesus' name.

> **Proverbs 3:32** "For the froward *is* abomination to the Lord......"

> **Proverbs 12:8** "A man shall be condemned according to his wisdom: but he that is of a perverse heart shall be despised."

Proverbs 28:18 "Whoso walketh uprightly shall be saved: but *he that* is <u>perverse</u> *in his* ways shall fall at once."

Heavenly Father, I thank you that according to Proverbs 28:18 my child shall walk not fall but shall walk upright before you and be saved. I thank you that my child shall not be despised because his/her heart shall not be perverted. Lord I ask you to protect my child's heart that he/she will not be seduced into perverted thinking or lifestyles In Jesus' name.

REJECTION

Common areas: Rejected by mother or father, rejection from the womb, rejected by peers, rejected by family, rejected by the opposite sex

I declare that my child is not rejected and that the spirit of rejection will not take root in my child's heart

I decree that every spirit of rejection trying to gain access to my child's life is removed in the name of Jesus.

> **I Peter 2:4** "Coming to Him *as to* a living stone, rejected indeed by men, but chosen by God *and* precious, ^{5} you also, as living stones, are being built up a spiritual house, a holy priesthood, to offer up spiritual sacrifices acceptable to God through Jesus Christ."

Heavenly Father, I thank you that the spirit of rejection is not rooted in the heart of my child. But Father I thank you that every demonic seed linked to rejection is removed and cast out of my child's life. I now rebuke every spirit of rejection that will try and gain access to my child because you said in Your word that You have accepted my child and You call him/her precious. Father I ask you that you fill my child's heart with Your love in Jesus' name. Amen.

ANGER

Common areas: generational anger, angry at parents/caregivers, angry with God, angry towards all adults and authority

I declare that power of anger is my child's life is broken by the blood of Jesus Christ.

I decree that my child will not be bound by the spirit of anger and that he/she is free from anger in Jesus' name.

> **Ephesians 4:26** "Be angry, and do not sin":[a] do not let the sun go down on your wrath, "

Lord, according to your word in Ephesians 4:26 we are not to sin because of anger or remain angry so God I thank you that my child is not angry. Lord because of your peace my child does not have to sin because of anger or remain angry. I thank you that the door to the spirit of anger is closed as I take authority over my child in Jesus' name Amen.

OCCULT

Common areas: ancestors, horoscopes, Ouija boards, psychics, tarot cards, witchcraft, sorcery, séances, mediums, clairvoyants, palm readers, or entertainment [books, music and television that promotes: witches, warlocks, psychics, and demonic powers etc.,]

I declare that spirits of the occult will not lure my child into darkness and my child will not be a worker of wickedness.

I decree that my child will not be made blind to the truth of Jesus Christ because of spirits of the occult.

Isaiah 47:13 "You are wearied with your many counsels; Let now the astrologers, Those who prophesy by the stars, Those who predict by the new moons, Stand up and save you from what will come upon you."

Leviticus 20:6 "As for the person who turns to mediums and to spiritists, to play the harlot after them, I will also set My face against that person and will cut him off from among his people. "

Leviticus 19:31 "Do not turn to mediums or spiritists; do not seek them out to be defiled by them. I am the LORD your God."

Deuteronomy 18:10-11 "There shall not be found among you anyone who makes his son or his daughter pass through the fire, one who uses divination, one who practices witchcraft, or one who interprets omens, or a sorcerer, or one who casts a spell, or a medium, or a spiritist, or one who calls up the dead."

Isaiah 8:19 "When they say to you, "Consult the mediums and the spiritists who whisper and mutter," should not a people consult their God? Should they consult the dead-on behalf of the living?"

Lord, you have spoken in Your Word over and over against demonic and occultic practices and I pray that you would keep my child's heart and mind in Christ Jesus that he/she would not be lured into darkness by spirits of the occult. I cover my child with the blood of Jesus that he/she will not be subtly seduced by occultic spirits through mediums of entertainment. Lord I also renounce, rebuke and come out of agreement with all generational spirits of the occult coming through the bloodline. I cast out of the bloodline all generational spirits of the occult linked to my ancestor's rebellion and wickedness in Jesus' name. Amen.

REBELLION

Common areas: Rebellion against parents, rebellion against authority, rebellion against God and His Word, rebellion against societal norms

I declare that rebellion, stubbornness, self-will, and disobedience will not cause my child to rebel against authority, societal norms, God and His Word or even his/her parents.

> **Psalm 107:11** "Because they had rebelled against the words of God And spurned the counsel of the Most High"

Purpose Driven Parenting

16

Purpose Driven Parenting can be defined as a parenting model that intentionally drives children towards their purpose. Purpose Driven Parenting deals with the tri-part (body, soul, and spirit) in order to push our children towards living a purpose driven life. With purpose driven parenting their gifts, talents, personality, weaknesses and strengths all play a role to ensure they are growing into their "purpose". Purpose driven parenting allows us to take the unfinished product to mold it into the desired finished product. Taking the time to deal with every aspect of their life in order to strengthen, fine tune or even correct flaws so they can continuously grow and develop into a well-rounded individual.

Ironically, in life we create vision boards, set goals and objectives for our career, business, and even our ministry so why wouldn't we do that and more for our children. Our children rely on us to prepare and equip them to be able to flourish in adulthood both naturally and spiritually so we must do this with great intention. Parenting is a lot of work and we all know that children do not come with an individualized instruction manual. *From birth to early adulthood is our window as parents to disciple, nurture their personalities, cultivate their gifts and help them maximize their talents*. This is why parents should consider a personal development plan for their children. Most of the time this concept is seen it is dealing with children with behavioral issues or special services for children that need extra help. But a personal development plan is a great tool that allows parents to set goals and objectives, and a course of action for their children and it also allows them to monitor progress and areas of improvement. Overall, creating a personal development plan for your child allows you to intentionally ensure that they are growing and developing into their "purpose". Nothing happens by accident so we can rest assured that if our children are nurtured and properly developed it was from intentional parenting. There are a number of things that should be considered when it comes to creating a personal development plan for your child, I have only listed 5 of these things below.

1. Gifts (I Corinthians 12) What spiritual gifts has the Lord purposed for your child? This is important because their gifts have a lot to do with the calling, mandate and assignment that God has for their life. It is important to nurture their gifts and keep them in a setting where they can grow and mature into their gifts. One of the best places to be able to safely grow in their gifts is at home under the supervision of their parents.

2. Talents: What innate ability does your child have that comes very naturally (i.e. singing, dancing, playing an instrument etc.,) Parents should ensure that talents are developed with relevant teachings, classes, and trainings.

3. Likes/Dislikes: What does your child like and dislike. It is

important to pay attention to things that interests them.

4. Strengths: What strengths does your child have as a person (i.e. outgoing personality, organized, compassionate towards other). Strengths are the areas where you child is flourishing and does not need as much attention.

5. Weaknesses: It is important to pay attention to our child's weaknesses and personality flaws (anger, isolated, socially awkward, sneaky etc.,) Weaknesses are areas of focus that require correction and monitoring. Overtime you will want to check for potential growth and improvements in these areas.

NOTE: I have included a template you can use to develop a personal development plan for your children. Feel free to adjust or make changes that best suit the needs of your children.

D'Andrea M. Bolden

Personal Development Plan Template

17

Date:

Child's Name:

Age:

Talents:
1. List Talent
2. List Talent
3. List Talent

Spiritual Gifts:
1. List Spiritual Gifts
2. List Spiritual Gifts
3. List Spiritual Gifts

Talents Development:
Action to help develop your child's talent. [Classes, workshops, trainings etc.,]

Gifts Development:
Come up with a plan to help develop your child their spiritual gifts.

Hobbies:
1. List Hobby

2. List Hobby
3. List Hobby

Encourage hobbies that your children enjoy and that are positive and leave them with a sense of fulfillment.

Academic strengths and interests: In regard to learning what does your child enjoy and what is a strong area.

Strengths : Summarize and list the strengths of your child.

Areas needing improvement: What areas do you see that require improvement. [Behavior, grades, organization etc.,]

Areas of focus:

Areas of focus are things that need to be prioritized and require attention.

20XX-20XX Goals:

For younger children as a parent you can set goals and objectives but the older your child gets they should begin to set realistic goals and objective for their own lives.

Immediate Goal:

Short term goals. Things that need to be or that will be accomplished quickly.

Activations!!

18

As parents we have spiritual authority over our children, particularly the father. It is important that we personally take the time to empower our children and begin to "activate" or get them active in spiritual things. Our children are more than capable of learning how to pray, learning the Word of God or even learning to discern the voice of the Lord. This chapter gives applicable tips to assist parents in the spiritual development of their children.

Baptism of the Holy Spirit

The baptism of the Holy Spirit is essential for every believer. It is the Holy spirit that empowers us to do the work of the Lord (Acts 1:8). The baptism of the Holy Spirit is a gift to every believer that ask in faith to receive. Jesus told the disciples not to hinder the children from coming to Him and this holds true to this day (Matthew 19:14). Jesus wants to be close even to the children. The baptism of the Holy Spirit is not just for adults but also for children.

Below are 6 tips to help prepare your children to receive the baptism of the Holy Spirit:

1. **Ensure they are ready and desire to receive the baptism of the Holy Spirit**. A resistant child is usually not the best candidate to receive the gift of the Holy Spirit. It

is important that the child is ready to receive because there is no particular age it all has to do with the readiness of that particular child. We have to surrender and willingly desire the indwelling of the Holy Spirit.

2. **Teach them** about the Holy Spirit and why as believer we need this awesome gift. Read scriptures that pertain to the baptism of the Holy Spirit. (Acts 2:4 etc.,)

3. **Kill fear**. Sometimes children for whatever reason can be fearful and this will shut down their ability to receive the baptism of the Holy Spirit. Sharing your own experience and reassuring them usually helps to calm their fears.

4.**Pray with them** so that their heart becomes ready to receive. Pray against fear or anything else that would block their ability to receive the baptism of the Holy Spirit

5. **Answer any question**s and/or address any concerns your child(ren) might have.

6. **Explain to them** how they might begin to speak words that do not sound familiar but that it is ok because the Holy Spirit wants to give them a new language.

Identify Spiritual gifts

Everyone is born with spiritual gifts that are assigned to them according to the will of God for their lives. When I mention spiritual gifts, I am only referring to the 9 gifts outlined in I Corinthians 12. These 9 gifts are supernatural manifestations of the Holy Spirit through the life of believers. The 9 spiritual gifts should not be confused with talents. Talents are innate abilities that an individual might have which in many cases can be anointed for service (i.e. singing, dancing, playing an instrument, drawing etc.,)

> Now concerning spiritual gifts, brethren, I would not have you ignorant. 2 Ye know that ye were Gentiles, carried away unto these dumb idols, even as ye were led. 3 Wherefore I give you to understand, that no man speaking by the Spirit of God calleth Jesus accursed: and that no man can say that Jesus is the Lord, but by the Holy Ghost. 4 Now there are diversities of gifts, but the same Spirit. 5 And there are differences of administrations, but the same Lord. 6 And there are diversities of operations, but it is the same God which worketh all in all. 7 But the manifestation of the Spirit is given to every man to profit withal. 8 For to one is given by the Spirit the word of wisdom; to another the word of knowledge by the same Spirit; 9 To another faith by the same Spirit; to another the gifts of healing by the same Spirit; 10 To another the working of miracles; to another prophecy; to another discerning of spirits; to another divers kinds of tongues; to another the interpretation of tongues: 11 But all these worketh that one and the selfsame Spirit, dividing to every man severally as he will. 12 For as the body is one, and hath many members, and all the members of that one body, being many, are one body: so also is Christ." - **I Corinthians 12:1-12**

*Listed below are four keys that can assist parents in identifying the spiritual gifts of their children:

Raising Prophets & Prophetic Types

1. **What are they drawn to?** Sometimes just paying attention to their spiritual appetites can give us insight into their spiritual gifts. Is your child drawn to the prophetic? Does your child get excited to pray for the sick?

2. **What has God spoken?** As parents it is our duty and responsibility to seek the Lord concerning the destiny of our children. We can seek out no better source and get no better answer than what comes from our Heavenly Father. Spend time in prayer and ask God to reveal what gifts have been given to your children.

3. **What has God revealed to them?** Many children including my own may begin to dream very early on and sometimes in these dreams God is revealing things to them that are relevant to what gifts He has given to them. As parents we should always talk to our children about their dreams to recognize if God is revealing some important truths.

4. **What gifts run strong in your family?** Many times, certain spiritual gifts run in our family. The gift of healing or even miracles could be a gift that runs in your family and there is a chance this same gift could also be in your children.

> "When I call to remembrance the unfeigned faith that is in thee, which dwelt first in thy grandmother Lois, and thy mother Eunice; and I am persuaded that in thee also." - **II Timothy 1:5**

Activate them in prayer

The bible says that man should always pray (Luke 18:1, I Thessalonians 5:16-18). Prayer is quintessential to our relationship with God along with our spiritual maturity and growth. This is why it is important that we teach our children how to pray. It is important that your Spirit filled child has an active prayer life. Learning to pray is what helps a child learn how to properly communicate with God and build a relationship.

Listed below are 5 tips for teaching children to pray:

1. Explain to them what prayer is as well as God's purpose for prayer.
Prayer is a vehicle that allows us to communicate with our heavenly prayer. Prayer is the medium that allows us to verbally release God's will in the earth.

2. Let them hear you pray out loud
It is important that our children hear and see us active in prayer. As parents our greatest audience is our children and we must lead by example.

3. Pray with them but encourage them to begin to lead in prayer
As children are learning to pray it is important to pray with them and as they become more comfortable allow them to begin "leading" in prayer and taking more of a lead role. This will build their confidence and it allows them to learn to pray with a greater level of independence.

4. Show them in the Word what God says about prayer

It is always important to know what God's word says about a particular matter. Because prayer is such an important part of our walk as believers that are plenty of scriptures about prayer. Listed below are several scriptural passages on prayer.

> Be careful for nothing; but in everything by prayer and supplication with thanksgiving let your requests be made known unto God. -**Philippians 4:6**

> Therefore I say unto you, What things soever ye desire, when ye pray, believe that ye receive [them], and ye shall have [them].- **Mark 11:24**

> Pray without ceasing. **1 Thessalonians 5:17**

> But when ye pray, use not vain repetitions, as the heathen [do]: for they think that they shall be heard for their much speaking.- **Matthew 6:7**

> Watch and pray, that ye enter not into temptation: the spirit indeed [is] willing, but the flesh [is] weak.- **Matthew 26:41**

> Confess [your] faults one to another, and pray one for another, that ye may be healed. The effectual fervent prayer of a righteous man availeth much.- **James 5:16**

> Call unto me, and I will answer thee, and shew thee great and mighty things, which thou knowest not.- **Jeremiah 33:3**

> Praying always with all prayer and supplication in the Spirit, and watching thereunto with all perseverance and supplication for all saints;- **Ephesians 6:18**
>
> And he spake a parable unto them [to this end], that men ought always to pray, and not to faint;- **Luke 18:1**

Exercise # 1: [Accelerated Prayer] You can do this with either just you and your children or with a small group. The goal is to have each person pray around a prayer point (family, protection, healing etc.) for about 20 seconds and then go on to the next person do this a few times to allow each person the opportunity to pray multiple times.

This will allow them a chance to pray in a group and become more confident. It will also teach them how to pray with focus by having a prayer point.

Exercise # 2: Pick a simple scripture that is easy for them to understand and show them how to pray the Word of God back to the Father. When we pray God's word, we echo back to him what he has already spoken, we also add more authority and strength to our prayer. Praying God's word allows us to be in agreement with what He has already spoken.

Try this using the scripture below

> For I know the plans I have for you," declares the LORD, "plans to prosper you and not to harm you, plans to give you hope and a future – **Jeremiah 29:11**

5. Allow them room to pray about what is in their heart.
I can remember when my daughter was younger, she would pray for Dora, Back Yardigans and any other cartoon pal she could think of because at that age she did not know any better. This type of behavior is normal for younger children. Now that she is older, she knows to pray for things that are appropriate and realistic and because she knows the voice of the Lord she is sensitive enough to be more led by His Spirit in prayer.

The Lord desires for our children to seek Him and know Him from the place of prayer.

Activate them in the prophetic

Teaching and training children in the prophetic is one of the most exciting things for me to do. Their innocence, willingness and curiosity are always a blessing to me. Children are no less capable of operating in the prophetic than adults. God desires to use our children just as much if not more than He desires to use you and me. Activating your child in the prophetic is not a difficult thing but it does take patience. When handling children you do not want to "quench their fire" in other words avoid being harsh and discouraging them. Allow them room to grow in this area they are children and are still learning His language.

Here are the 4 Keys to Activating Your Child in the Prophetic

1. Any child desiring to prophesy should be Spirit filled

because the baptism of the Holy Spirit is the prerequisite [Acts 19:6].

2. Take the time to explain and define prophecy to your child. [Simple definition: Prophecy is speaking and revealing God's heart and will for a specific persons(s) or place(s).] Consider the age and level of maturity because sometimes simpler works best. Be sure to explain things at a level that is appropriate for your child. Just explain the basics no need to go too far in depth right away especially with younger children. It is better to let them grow in their prophetic grace and continue teaching them as they grow in order to avoid overwhelming them. Make sure they understand that prophecy should build, exhort and edify God's people and is not to be used to cause harm in any sort of way.

But he that prophesieth speaketh unto men to edification, and exhortation, and comfort. – [**I Corinthians 14:3**]

3. Ensure that they understand that they can PROPHESY [I Corinthians 14:31]. Many times children can be a bit fearful, bashful or just unsure but most of the time they are willing so reiterate that they CAN PROPHESY.
I would that ye all spake with tongues, but rather that ye prophesied: for greater is he that prophesieth than he that speaketh with tongues, except he interpret, that the church may receive edifying. *[I Corinthians 14:5]*

For you can all prophesy in turn so that everyone may be instructed and encouraged. *[I Corinthians 14:31]*

4. Activate their faith and allow them to begin to share what God is saying to them. Times of prayer and quiet times of reading the Word are great opportunities to activate your child in the prophetic. Their ability to hear can be hindered for a number of reasons. They must learn how to quiet down and take the time to receive what the Holy Spirit is releasing to their Spirit. Some children will "see" the Word of the Lord in images, visions, words etc., while others may primarily hear the Word of the Lord and this is totally normal.

Exercise: [Simple prophetic word] Have your child pray and ask the Holy Spirit to speak one word to them and then have them share what He is saying

Be sure to continue to build their faith and encourage them to desire to prophesy. It is important for them to understand the role faith plays in the prophetic. They must have faith and believe that God will use them to prophesy. Ultimately our level of faith can affect our prophetic abilities.

Wherefore, brethren, covet to prophesy, and forbid not to speak with tongues. *[I Corinthians 14:39]*

Having then gifts differing according to the grace that is given to us, whether prophecy, let us prophesy according to the proportion of faith; *[Romans 12:6]*

Conclusion

As parents we have such a simple yet complex job of raising our children. There is no perfect child nor is there a perfect way to raise children. Every child has a different personality and way of handling things so two siblings could be absolutely nothing alike. We can only stand on the Word of God and apply wisdom as we handle our children. I believe parenting is a humbling job because we have to go back to God in prayer many times because we do not understand how to handle our children or why they are acting a certain way. God knows and understands our children much better than we ever could so prayer is a must for every parent. It is our job to disciple our children to the best of our ability in our homes. As parents we are like their personal guards watching over them and making sure they are alright.

No matter how challenging parenting can be we have an assignment to complete. This is why we have to continuously see our children as our priority ministry. We must cultivate and develop our children like a flower garden, giving them all of the necessary care to ensure healthy growth. I have such a love for children and a strong desire to see them excel and succeed in all areas of their lives. My heart's desire is for children to be used by God just like adults. I want to see children who are healthy and happy loving on the Lord. I pray that God would continue to give us wisdom, knowledge, and understanding to handle all of the blessings He has given us in the form of children.

Section 2

Young Prophetic Artists: God's Forgotten Creatives

Introduction

Prophetically gifted children are born with a special combination of gifts, talents and abilities that make them some of the most unique, creative, and innovative individuals. The supernatural grace on their life allows their innate talents and abilities to become exceptional and above average.

Prophetically gifted children many times are also very gifted in the arts and have an innate ability to excel in these areas beyond the norm. So, it is not shocking that some of the world's greatest poets, chefs, painters, graphic designers, dancers, musicians, songwriters, builders, jewelry designers, fashion designers, playwrights, authors and singers are prophetically gifted.

Prophetic sensitivity linked with creativity, fuels their spontaneous inspiration and ability to create art. Creating new art and bringing vision to manifestation gives them a sense of happiness. The inability to create and birth new art causes many artists to become depressed. Sadly, some artists have tried to use drugs or even the occult in order to become inspired to produce art. These dangerous tactics have ruined lives as many have suffered the consequences of opening the door to addiction, mental illness, and demonic torment.

When artists experience a lack of creativity many times it is because they are not connected to God. God is the true source and originator of creativity and He never runs out of new things for man to create. On the other hand, no matter how in tune we are with God there will be seasons that are not filled with as much inspiration and outward productivity. As parents it is imperative that we teach our children to stay connected to God because He has the plan for their life. This is important because many artists do not realize that their skill and wisdom comes from God and should be used to glorify Him. A lot of artists begin to become prideful and self-exalted as they feel that their abilities are because of their own strength.

The creativity, wisdom and insight given to prophetically gifted people is astounding as it has helped to continuously progress the spheres of influence in the earth. The fact that many people do not recognize these gifts and abilities in themselves let alone their children does not negate the fact that they exist. These supernaturally gifted individuals have a divine purpose and plan that is ordained by God.

D'Andrea M. Bolden

Art & Creativity-1

"Art is a collaboration between God and the artist, and the less the artist does the better" – **Andre Gide**

Creativity & GOD

1. the use of the imagination or original ideas, especially in the production of an artistic work.

We serve the God of creation. And creativity belongs to our God. It's amazing how when God created man in His image this included the ability for man to use their imaginations, be creative, and create. Our all-powerful God showed the power of His creativity beginning in Genesis the first chapter.

> In the beginning God created the heaven and the earth. And the earth was without form, and void; and darkness was upon the face of the deep. And the Spirit of God moved upon the face of the waters. And God said, Let there be light: and there was light. And God saw the light, that it was good: and God divided the light from the darkness. And God called the light Day, and the darkness he called Night. And the evening and the morning were the first day. And God said, Let there be a firmament in the midst of the waters, and let it divide the waters from the waters. And God made the firmament, and divided the waters

which were under the firmament from the waters which were above the firmament: and it was so.
- **Genesis 1:1-7**

Creativity & Imagination

Our imaginations when pure will allow us to showcase the creative side and nature of our creator. When our imaginations our fueled by righteous thoughts the things we imagine and create will be righteous. The only danger with our imagination is when our hearts and minds become demonically influenced. This will cause us to use our creativity to imagine and create things that are wicked. Creativity belongs to God, but the imitation and perversion of creativity belongs to the enemy.

> *And God saw that the wickedness of man was great in the earth, and that every imagination of the thoughts of his heart was only evil continually.*
> - **Genesis 6:5**

Creativity is not a strength for everyone and there are multiples reasons for this. Many people are just not as creative while others might have had their imaginations and creativity killed as a child. As parents we want to give our kids room to be creative but we also cannot allow their creativity and imaginations to run wild without safe boundaries.

The Power of Creativity

Creativity births; new songs, movies, plays, fashion designs, building types, paintings, illustrations, choreography, lyrics, photos, poems, and graphic designs. Creativity is the engine that produces; new ideas, new inventions, new designs, new business models, new technology, new medical advancements and so forth. Without creativity in the earth in the form of people life would lack many of the things we have come to love. Without creativity there would be no cartoons, crayons, colorful toys, flat-screen televisions, custard filled cupcakes, great smelling perfume, beautiful diamond rings, high-end fabrics and anything else that comes to your creative mind.

If you have a child that is drawn to the arts find the area that they are best skilled and invest in classes or workshops that will help them master their skillset. There is nothing wrong with mastering one's talent but there has to be talent in the area you are trying to help your child master. When children are operating in the area that they skilled in they will enjoy the things they are doing.

Art is just one of the many ways God can release His creativity in the earth. Art communicates a message and leaves an impression in the lives of people. God wants to release His message and be glorified through art. We have all seen enough of the enemy's "art" such as statutes of false gods, pornography, X-rated cartoons, satanic temples, demonic paintings and so forth. The secular world especially those in the occult understand and appreciate art and the power it has. It is time for artists to be reconnected with their Heavenly Father. As we disciple the next generation of prophetic artists, we have a charge to help them partner their talent with the prophetic. This will allow them to be led by the Holy Spirit and keep their message pure.

When it comes to the prophetic some people hear more and others "see more. The prophetic can be visual or auditory and this also holds true with many forms of art. So, when an individual that is skilled in the arts is able to be in tune with what the Holy Spirit is sharing with them it can come out in their art. For instance, the Holy Spirit might show a painter a beautiful image and then using their skill as an artist they can draw and paint this image and it is now tangible in the earth. A songwriter or music producer can hear a song in their sleep, and with their skillset they can record the lyrics and help produce the music to accompany the lyrics. A fashion designer can easily be inspired by colors, textures and fabrics in order to create new garments and clothing. It is important that artists learn what inspires them and the way God speaks to them. This will aide them in following the leading and promptings of the Holy Spirit.

God's Forgotten Creatives-2

God has been restoring gifts, functions and anointings in the body of Christ for quite a while. Although God has been restoring the prophetic and the function of the prophet back to the church, we have limited how God can release creatively through prophetic people. The ability to be prophetically expressive outside of "thus saith the Lord" and musically in the form of worship has left no room for a large number of prophetic people. There is a myriad of creative and prophetic people that have been misplaced and even outright forgotten in the body of Christ. When we begin to realize God does not equip people with great skill and ability for no reason, we will then begin to realize the need for them to understand and find their purpose.

Creativity, Wisdom, & Skill

There is a skill and wisdom that accompanies those that are creative. Artistic creativity is God given and although some things can be taught others cannot. All throughout the scriptures we can read about how God gave wisdom, skill and creativity to people to create a variety of things. The things in scripture that were created ranged from garments to structures. Below are some scriptures that reference many skilled artistic types.

Master builders, Architects, Skilled workers

*You have many workers: stonecutters, masons and carpenters, as well as those **skilled** in every kind of work* – **I Chronicles 22:15 (NIV)**

Clothes makers, Fashion Designers, Masters of garments

*Tell all the **skilled** workers to whom I have given **wisdom** in such matters that they are to make garments for Aaron, for his consecration, so he may serve me as priest.* – **Exodus 28:3 (NIV)**

Craftsman, Woodworking, Jewelry makers, etc.,

*and I have filled him with the Spirit of God, with **wisdom**, with understanding, with knowledge and with all kinds of **skills**— **to make artistic designs** for work in gold, silver and bronze, to cut and set stones, to work in wood, and to engage in all kinds of crafts.* - **Exodus 31:3 (NIV)**

Tapestry, Weavers, Knitters, Fashion Crafts & Designers, Embroidery, Engravers, etc.

*He has filled them with **skill** to do all kinds of work as engravers, designers, embroiderers in blue, purple*

*and scarlet yarn and fine linen, and weavers--all of them **skilled** workers and **designers**.*
– Exodus 35:35 (NIV)

Every skilled woman spun with her hands and brought what she had spun--blue, purple or scarlet yarn or fine linen. **– Exodus 35:25 (NIV)**

Pottery & Ceramics

Then I went down to the potter's house, and, behold, he wrought a work on the wheels. And the vessel that he made of clay was marred in the hand of the potter: so he made it again another vessel, as seemed good to the potter to make it. **– Jeremiah 18:3-4**

Perfume Makers, Chefs, Bakers, Culinary Arts

He will take your daughters to be perfumers and cooks and bakers. **– I Samuel 8:13**

Writers & Poets

Oh, that my words were recorded, that they were written on a scroll, that they were inscribed with an iron tool on lead, or engraved in rock forever!
– Job 19:23-24

Singers, Spoken Word Artists, Poets

My heart is stirred by a noble theme as I recite my verses for the king; my tongue is the pen of a skillful writer. – **Psalm 45:1(b)**

For in him we live and move and have our being.' As some of your own poets have said, 'We are his offspring. – **Acts 17:28**

Singers, Musicians, Songwriters, Composers, Producers

And David spake to the chief of the Levites to appoint their brethren to be the singers with instruments of musick, psalteries and harps and cymbals, sounding, by lifting up the voice with joy. **-I Chronicles 15:16**

Praise the Lord! Praise God in his sanctuary; praise him in his mighty heavens! Praise him for his mighty deeds; praise him according to his excellent greatness! Praise him with trumpet sound; praise him with lute and harp! Praise him with tambourine and dance; praise him with strings and pipe! Praise him with sounding cymbals; praise him with loud clashing cymbals – **Psalm 150:1-6**

Sing to him a new song; play skillfully on the strings, with loud shouts – **Psalm 33:3**

I will sing to the Lord as long as I live; I will sing praise to my God while I have being. – **Psalm 104:33**

Make a joyful noise to the Lord, all the earth; break forth into joyous song and sing praises! - **Psalm 98:4**

He put a new song in my mouth, a song of praise to our God. Many will see and fear, and put their trust in the Lord. – **Psalm 40:3**

And when the builders laid the foundation of the temple of the Lord, the priests in their vestments came forward with trumpets, and the Levites, the sons of Asaph, with cymbals, to praise the Lord, according to the directions of David king of Israel. – **Ezra 3:10**

Praise the Lord! Sing to the Lord a new song, his praise in the assembly of the godly! – **Psalm 149:1**

Praise the Lord! For it is good to sing praises to our God; for it is pleasant, and a song of praise is fitting. – **Psalm 147:1**

Prophetic Expression-3

Expression
1. The process of making one's thoughts or feelings known

The prophetic is a form of expression that allows God's thoughts and feelings to be made known. Prophetic people are the instruments that God uses to express himself in the earth. There are a variety of ways God can use man to express Himself.

"For no prophecy was ever produced by the will of man, but men spoke from God as they were carried along by the Holy Spirit." **2 Peter 1:21**

Sadly, prophetic artists are not seen as prophetic or God inspired for the most part in the church. This has caused many to leave the church or suppress their talents because what they have to offer has not been received or appreciated. When we take the limits off of God and how He can use people we will realize that many everyday talents and skills can serve a "higher" purpose. God doesn't give us extraordinary artistic talents and abilities with no reason or purpose in mind. The purpose of art like anything else is not simply to make money but to glorify God. Understanding this can help us reach the next generation of prophetic artists so that they can embrace their identity in Christ Jesus.

We need to understand that God can get his message across in many ways. This allows His message to reach more people. If all we do is stand in a mic and prophesy at church, we will miss the people at the art gallery, theater, fashion shows and so forth. God can raise up and use pure prophetic vessels to show off His creative nature through art. This can be done in a way that will draw unbelievers that are lovers of art. It can also allow people to see God's heart towards art. If there are artists that hear the voice of the Lord, they are able to connect with and reach other artists. The standard and the bar for artists can be raised as people begin to see powerful Spirit-filled artists.

Prophetic Flow-4

Many highly talented youth that are very creative in artistic expression are many times troubled and prone to be drawn to demonic activity. This happens because they "see" the world very different and are many times misunderstood. Prophetic artists are visually gifted by nature and prone to see strong dreams and visions and this is what many times motivates their creativity. When this is not recognized it leaves an open door for demonic harassment and visitations which can eventually be conveyed in their art. But if they are discipled and Spirit-filled we can begin to harness and groom their prophetic stream of dreams and visions.

Dreams & Visions

It is quite common for prophetic children to have strong dreams and visions. Anyone that has a strong prophetic call will have to be able to receive and process divine revelation. This is why God begins to awaken many prophetic people during their childhood. Although God is speaking to many of them like the prophet Samuel, they need someone to help them recognize His voice (1 Samuel 3:1-21). As parents, it is imperative that we know the voice of the Lord so that we will be able to recognize when He is speaking to our children. Once they recognize how God speaks to them this can be connected to their innate artistic talents and you will find they can draw and paint what God has shown them. Ultimately this allows them to use their talents, yield their minds and glorify God. They are born to express through art what God has shown them through a pure heart. Just think about if Ezekiel could have drawn the wheel in the middle of the wheel.

Prophetic Artists-5

When art is inspired by God, God is the artist and man is just the vessel. A prophetic artist just yields his or herself to use their skillset to release what the Holy Spirit is downloading. As the Holy Spirit inspires and breathes on the artistic vessel, their job is to receive the download. Prophetic artists many times are inspired by things around them in their environment. Being inspired by what is around you (environment) is an example of external stimuli. Your imagination, innate creativity and the leading of the Holy Spirit are considered internal stimuli. Internal and external stimuli can work together, separately or even co-dependently. Below is a limited list of different types of artists.

Singers – When anointed they can make great psalmists that are able to release the heart of the Father in song. Many can also write songs or play instruments as well. When they partner their talent to sing with the prophetic they can release prophetic songs.

Musicians – Musicians are skilled in the playing of instruments to make rhythms and sounds. When anointed many are powerful minstrels. Minstrels can move the hand of God and (II Kings 3:15). Minstrels have the ability to release prophetic music. As they open their prophetic ears they are able to play as led by the Spirit. Many minstrels also sing and are prolific songwriters.

Songwriters – Songwriters will write lyrics or the music that goes to a song. Songwriters are masters of song as they are able to write lyrics for singers or music for minstrels. When they are tuned in to heaven they have the capacity to receive new songs from heaven that will be released in the earth.

Playwrights & Filmmakers – Playwrights & Filmmakers have the uncanny ability to take real life or even fictitious scenarios and produce high-energy performances. They are at their best when they are Spirit-filled and flowing in a way that their films and plays can be used as evangelistic tools.

Painters & Visual Artists – Painters and visual artists are easily inspired by what is around them. They will capture what they see around them or what they can imagine. When led by the Holy Spirit they will be able to receive inspiration from God and then use their skill to make it into art.

Poets & Spoken Word Artists – Poets and spoken word artists are gifted in not just words by the delivery of them. Poets and spoken word artists have a way of bringing words to life. Their voice intonation and inflection, body movements and animation are what make them stand out.

Writers- Writers are the pens of the Lord. They can write and record what the Lord is saying. Writers use their creativity to prophetically express themselves in the written form. They are unique as their abilities can allow them to do a variety of things. Many writers will pen books, songs, movies, plays, poems and so forth.

Dancers – Dancers understand the power of movement. By design they can express ideas, concepts and even emotions without saying one word. Dance is a form of visual art that showcases inspired, choreographed and spontaneous movements that many times convey a very powerful message.

Photographers – They literally see life through a different lens (pun intended). Photographers are able to not just take photos but to capture life, moments and tell stories through their visual art.

Graphic Designers – Graphic designers are creative geniuses that can conceptualize how to bring inanimate objects to life (books, cd, product packaging, business logo). A graphic designer can make a visual of how an event, business, or ministry should "look". Graphic designers are skilled in using colors, lighting, text and images to give a visual personality to an idea, organization or even a product. They understand how to blend together text, colors, and images to create a visual presentation that communicates to the audience. For example, a graphic designer understands how to silently speak to book readers. They can create a book cover that embodies the title and feel of the book in order to connect the book to its audience. Graphic designers with their talents are what helps to make life "look" good. Many graphic designers have a strong prophetic grace on their life.

Fashion Designers – Fashion designers are very unique as they are strong visionaries with big imaginations. Fashion designers are inspired by colors, fabrics, and textures. They are very creative as they envision new designs and ideas. They are truly masters of garments as they have the ability to make people "look" good on the outside.

Other Types of Artists
Jewelry Designers
Chefs & Bakers
Perfume Makers
Architects & Master Builders
Choreographers
Woodworkers
Animators
Free-lance artists
Graffiti
Stained glass makers
Pottery and ceramics
Assemblage

Metalsmiths
Video
Tapestry
Furniture makers
Landscape and design
Interior Decorators
Drawing and sketch artists
Painters

Conclusion

As a final thought it is so imperative to give your prophetic artist a way to use their talents to glorify God. Like any other prophetic child, they must be discipled in the word of God as satan has an agenda to destroy every prophetic artist. Many of them lack understanding of what God has given them which, and this is why many of them are tormented and become bound with mental illness, addiction and perversion.

We have all seen how perverted and dark the work of artists can become when they have yielded their talents and minds to a wicked purpose. Satan understands how powerful these creative people are and this is why they must find their place in the earth. Any prophetic person that is disconnected from the Father and that has zero word in them is a target for satan. Satan will in turn infiltrate their dreams, visions and imagination with wickedness. The prophetic artists are destined for greatness and they have so much to share and as parents we have a job to do. They can no longer be ignored but must now be embraced because now is the time for the prophetic artists to RISE!!!!

Section 3

Prophetic children:
Dreams, Visions + Supernatural Encounters

Introduction

Is your child a dreamer? Does your child see visions? If so, do not ignore them. Although every dream or vision does not have any spiritual benefit we still need to listen to our children. This is so important because dreams and visions are the language of God. Every human being on the planet has the innate ability to receive divine communication from God especially in the form of a dream. The concept of dreams is fascinating and has researchers across the globe trying to find answers. Dreams are a language all their own and interpretation comes solely from our Heavenly Father. So, if your child is a dreamer you need to explain to them that God can speak to them through dreams. And take the time to show them scriptures about dreams. This will cause them to be more mindful and pay attention when they have dreams.

Remember in 1 Samuel the 3rd chapter God was speaking to Samuel, but he was young and did not yet know the voice of the Lord. Very often God is speaking to our children and it is up to us to teach them to recognize and respond to the voice of the Lord. Understand that not only will God communicate with children in dreams and visions the enemy will try and come with demonic communication. Many prophetic children that are dreamers battle with nightmares and being harassed at night by demonic spirits. Some children dream vividly almost every night and taking the time to listen to their dreams can give some insight to the source of their dreams or even reveal a message that God has been speaking through dreams. The first half of this book is geared towards you, the parents and other adults that are responsible for prophetic children. The second half of this book is some activities for you to do along with your prophetic child.

D'Andrea M. Bolden

The Language of God-1

Language: a system of communication by speaking, writing, or making signs in a way that can be understood, or any of the different systems of communication used in particular regions or communities.[1]

Based on man's definition of a language God's language does not quite meet all our earthly expectations. We must remember that English, Spanish, Swahili, Braille, ASL or even German are languages for humans to communicate and interact, but the language of God precedes and is superior to man's methods of communication.

People typically speak through reading, writing, or even signs which are understood by natural means, but God will speak to our spirit. Because natural methods are the ways that we are most comfortable receiving communication, God will speak to us in a still small voice, through His servants, and even through His written Word. But dreams and visions are quite different because God can speak to our spirit and bypass our natural processes and understanding.

If the language of God were not different from other languages people would not be perplexed by the dreams and visions that they see but just like Pharaoh and King Nebuchadnezzar many do not recognize or even understand the way God speaks. When a message has been communicated in a language that you do not understand you will need to have the message translated. Translation allows a message to be converted from one language to another. Dream interpretation is the equivalent of translating a message from one language to another so that it can be understood. Because dreams and visions are a part of God's language and way of communication the interpretation and understanding also come from God.

Genesis 41:1-37 (Pharaoh's Dream)

"And it came to pass at the end of two full years, that Pharaoh dreamed: and, behold, he stood by the river. ² And, behold, there came up out of the river seven well favoured kine and fatfleshed; and they fed in a meadow. ³ And, behold, seven other kine came up after them out of the river, ill favoured and leanfleshed; and stood by the other kine upon the brink of the river. ⁴ And the ill favoured and leanfleshed kine did eat up the seven well favoured and fat kine. So, Pharaoh awoke. ⁵ And he slept and dreamed the second time: and, behold, seven ears of corn came up upon one stalk, rank and good. ⁶ And, behold, seven thin ears and blasted with the east wind sprung up after them. ⁷ And the seven thin ears devoured the seven rank and full ears. And Pharaoh awoke, and, behold, it was a dream. ⁸ And it came to pass in the morning that his spirit was troubled; and he sent and called for all the magicians of Egypt, and all the wise men thereof: and Pharaoh told them his dream; but there was none that could interpret them unto Pharaoh. ⁹ Then spake the chief butler unto Pharaoh, saying, I do remember my faults this day:

[10] Pharaoh was wroth with his servants, and put me in ward in the captain of the guard's house, both me and the chief baker: [11] And we dreamed a dream in one night, I and he; we dreamed each man according to the interpretation of his dream. [12] And there was there with us a young man, an Hebrew, servant to the captain of the guard; and we told him, and he interpreted to us our dreams; to each man according to his dream he did interpret. [13] And it came to pass, as he interpreted to us, so it was; me he restored unto mine office, and him he hanged. [14] Then Pharaoh sent and called Joseph, and they brought him hastily out of the dungeon: and he shaved himself, and changed his raiment, and came in unto Pharaoh. [15] And Pharaoh said unto Joseph, I have dreamed a dream, and there is none that can interpret it: and I have heard say of thee, that thou canst understand a dream to interpret it. [16] And Joseph answered Pharaoh, saying, It is not in me: God shall give Pharaoh an answer of peace. [17] And Pharaoh said unto Joseph, In my dream, behold, I stood upon the bank of the river: [18] And, behold, there came up out of the river seven kine, fatfleshed and well favoured; and they fed in a meadow: [19] And, behold, seven other kine came up after them, poor and very ill favoured and leanfleshed, such as I never saw in all the land of Egypt for badness: [20] And the lean and the ill favoured kine did eat up the first seven fat kine: [21] And when they had eaten them up, it could not be known that they had eaten them; but they were still ill

favoured, as at the beginning. So I awoke. ^{22} And I saw in my dream, and, behold, seven ears came up in one stalk, full and good: ^{23} And, behold, seven ears, withered, thin, and blasted with the east wind, sprung up after them: ^{24} And the thin ears devoured the seven good ears: and I told this unto the magicians; but there was none that could declare it to me. ^{25} And Joseph said unto Pharaoh, The dream of Pharaoh is one: God hath shewed Pharaoh what he is about to do. ^{26} The seven good kine are seven years; and the seven good ears are seven years: the dream is one. ^{27} And the seven thin and ill favoured kine that came up after them are seven years; and the seven empty ears blasted with the east wind shall be seven years of famine. ^{28} This is the thing which I have spoken unto Pharaoh: What God is about to do he sheweth unto Pharaoh. ^{29} Behold, there come seven years of great plenty throughout all the land of Egypt: ^{30} And there shall arise after them seven years of famine; and all the plenty shall be forgotten in the land of Egypt; and the famine shall consume the land; ^{31} And the plenty shall not be known in the land by reason of that famine following; for it shall be very grievous. ^{32} And for that the dream was doubled unto Pharaoh twice; it is because the thing is established by God, and God will shortly bring it to pass. ^{33} Now therefore let Pharaoh look out a man discreet and wise, and set him over the land of Egypt. ^{34} Let Pharaoh do this, and let him appoint officers over the land, and take up the fifth part of the land of Egypt in the seven plenteous years. ³⁵ And let them gather all the food of those good years that come, and lay up corn under the hand of Pharaoh, and let them keep food in the cities. ³⁶ And that food shall be for store to the land against the seven years of famine, which shall be in the land of Egypt; that the land perish not through the famine. ³⁷ And the thing was good in the eyes of Pharaoh, and in the eyes of all his servants."

Daniel 2: 1-46 (King Nebuchadnezzar's Dream)
"And in the second year of the reign of Nebuchadnezzar Nebuchadnezzar dreamed dreams, wherewith his spirit was troubled, and his sleep brake from him. ² Then the king commanded to call the magicians, and the astrologers, and the sorcerers, and the Chaldeans, for to shew the king his dreams. So they came and stood before the king. ³ And the king said unto them, I have dreamed a dream, and my spirit was troubled to know the dream. ⁴ Then spake the Chaldeans to the king in Syriack, O king, live for ever: tell thy servants the dream, and we will shew the interpretation. ⁵ The king answered and said to the Chaldeans, The thing is gone from me: if ye will not make known unto me the dream, with the interpretation thereof, ye shall be cut in pieces, and your houses shall be made a dunghill. ⁶ But if ye shew the dream, and the interpretation thereof, ye shall receive of me gifts and rewards and great honour: therefore shew me the dream, and the interpretation thereof. ⁷ They answered again and

interpretation thereof? ²⁷ Daniel answered in the presence of the king, and said, The secret which the king hath demanded cannot the wise men, the astrologers, the magicians, the soothsayers, shew unto the king; ²⁸ But there is a God in heaven that revealeth secrets, and maketh known to the king Nebuchadnezzar what shall be in the latter days. Thy dream, and the visions of thy head upon thy bed, are these; ²⁹ As for thee, O king, thy thoughts came into thy mind upon thy bed, what should come to pass hereafter: and he that revealeth secrets maketh known to thee what shall come to pass. ³⁰ But as for me, this secret is not revealed to me for any wisdom that I have more than any living, but for their sakes that shall make known the interpretation to the king, and that thou mightest know the thoughts of thy heart. ³¹ Thou, O king, sawest, and behold a great image. This great image, whose brightness was excellent, stood before thee; and the form thereof was terrible. ³² This image's head was of fine gold, his breast and his arms of silver, his belly and his thighs of brass, ³³ His legs of iron, his feet part of iron and part of clay. ³⁴ Thou sawest till that a stone was cut out without hands, which smote the image upon his feet that were of iron and clay, and brake them to pieces. ³⁵ Then was the iron, the clay, the brass, the silver, and the gold, broken to pieces together, and became like the chaff of the summer threshingfloors; and the wind carried them away, that no place was found for them: and the stone that smote the image became a great mountain, and filled the whole earth. [36] This is the dream; and we will tell the interpretation thereof before the king. [37] Thou, O king, art a king of kings: for the God of heaven hath given thee a kingdom, power, and strength, and glory. [38] And wheresoever the children of men dwell, the beasts of the field and the fowls of the heaven hath he given into thine hand, and hath made thee ruler over them all. Thou art this head of gold. [39] And after thee shall arise another kingdom inferior to thee, and another third kingdom of brass, which shall bear rule over all the earth. [40] And the fourth kingdom shall be strong as iron: forasmuch as iron breaketh in pieces and subdueth all things: and as iron that breaketh all these, shall it break in pieces and bruise. [41] And whereas thou sawest the feet and toes, part of potters' clay, and part of iron, the kingdom shall be divided; but there shall be in it of the strength of the iron, forasmuch as thou sawest the iron mixed with miry clay. [42] And as the toes of the feet were part of iron, and part of clay, so the kingdom shall be partly strong, and partly broken. [43] And whereas thou sawest iron mixed with miry clay, they shall mingle themselves with the seed of men: but they shall not cleave one to another, even as iron is not mixed with clay. [44] And in the days of these kings shall the God of heaven set up a kingdom, which shall never be destroyed: and the kingdom shall not be left to other people, but it shall break in pieces and consume all these kingdoms, and it shall stand for ever. [45] Forasmuch as thou sawest that the stone was cut out of the mountain without hands, and that it brake in pieces the iron, the brass, the clay, the silver, and the gold; the great God hath made known to the king what shall come to pass hereafter: and the dream is certain, and the interpretation thereof sure. [46] Then the king Nebuchadnezzar fell upon his face, and worshipped Daniel, and commanded that they should offer an oblation and sweet odours unto him."

Mastery of a new language typically takes years, but God's language is understood supernaturally and He can grace us with the ability to interpret what He is saying in dreams and visions. Sadly, many believers cannot understand when and what God is speaking if it is not written or audibly spoken. Because dreams and visions are a language by themselves many people are baffled about what they are seeing. When people do not understand their dreams or visions, they are prone to not pay attention or even assume it was just some weird happenstance. Throughout the bible we can read about people having dreams and visions. We can also read about the need for interpretation to come from God or even through those that are connected to our Heavenly Father.

Many times, God will begin dealing with prophetic children primarily through dreams and visions. I can attest to this truth because both of my children began to come to me about their dreams by 4 years of age. When your child begins to have dreams and visions they are being introduced to and immersed in a new language. They will need help and guidance to understand what is being spoken to them. The way we handle their dreams and visions will affect them in the years to come. For instance, if we constantly ignore our children when they are telling us about their dreams, they are prone to also begin ignoring their dreams. Taking the time to listen can make a world of difference. As parents, we might not always understand but we can always be a listening ear. We must be adamant on helping our children recognize when God is speaking to them. We will dive further into the topic of dreams in the next chapter.

Dreams-2

Dream: An encounter while sleep that many times engages our senses (sight, hearing, smell, taste and touch)

One of the major characteristics of a dream is that they occur when a person is asleep. When we are sleep, we are in many ways vulnerable. But we are also relaxed and quiet enough for God to speak to us without interruption.

> *Job 33:14-16* "For God may speak in one way, or in another, *Yet man* does not perceive it. [15] In a dream, in a vision of the night, When deep sleep falls upon men, While slumbering on their beds, [16] Then He opens the ears of men, And seals their instruction."

Looking at the verses above from the book of Job we can see that God is able to speak loud and clear when we are sleep. And many times, this happens in the form of a dream. I have yet to meet one person that has never had one dream. Every person created by God has the innate capacity to receive divine communication from Him in the form of a dream. Dreams from God are not limited to believers if this were the case God would have never spoke to Pharaoh and King Nebuchadnezzar in a dream.

Types of Dreams

Although many understand that dreams and visions are a way that God can speak to us, we also need to understand that there are different types of dreams.

Prophetic Dreams: A prophetic dream can be seen as a dream that needs no interpretation because what is seen is what happens. Many people are perplexed or even flabbergasted by having dreams that happen in real life. People have had dreams of wars, tragedies, or even personal experiences before they transpire. So, with prophetic dreams God can reveal and make one privy to circumstances, situations and experiences before they occur in real life.

Symbolic dreams: These dreams are also from God but are not as easily understood. These are dreams that require interpretation like the dreams of Pharaoh and King Nebuchadnezzar. Many times, in symbolic dreams the meaning is hidden but we can always seek God for interpretation and wisdom to understand what He is speaking in a dream. God can speak the same message in a dream, but it might not be the exact same dream. When dreams are symbolic there are many things to consider such as location, time of day, people, animals, numbers, colors, clothing and so forth. As it relates to dreams from God we cannot lean on our own understanding or intellect. Because God takes the foolish things and confounds the wise (I Corinthians 1:27). This is God's language so we must ask Him for understanding and interpretation.

Soulish dreams: Soulish dreams are dreams that can come from the soul and subconscious mind. Have you ever binge watched a TV show and then had a dream about the TV show? Are you afraid of spiders and keep having dreams about spiders? Some dreams can come from the overflow of our heart, our fears, past traumatic occurrences, sin or what we are indulging ourselves with on a regular basis. Some people that have endured traumatic events will keep seeing the event over and over in their dreams. Soulish dreams do not necessarily have a spiritual benefit although they can sometimes show us the dealings of our heart. Many things such as anger, sadness, or even fear can manifest in our dreams. Soulish dreams can convey the dealings of our heart and even the ponderings of the mind.

Demonic dreams: Unfortunately, the vulnerability of man at night when sleep does not end with God. Demons will cause nightmares, sexually explicit dreams, violent dreams, or even dreams that will seduce a person into sin. People have had dreams about getting drunk or getting high to the point they could taste the substance or even feel high in their dream. This is a tactic of satan to drag some people back into addiction or to seduce others into sin. Demonic dreams can be frightening and very intense. For many people, the assignment of demonic dreams is to plague individuals with the spirit of fear. This can also be very common with prophetic children.

Purpose of Dreams

The number one purpose of dreams is communication. God did not create us to be void of Him in every aspect of life. But just like a remote and television God wants to be able to communicate with us and the closer we are too Him the better communication will be for us. Through dreams God can release impartation, direction, warning, insight, witty inventions, strategies, answers to prayers, songs, or even a word for someone else. Some dreams are simply a means to prompt us to pray and intercede.

God wants to speak to us, and He has a lot to say to us and many times this is in the form of a dream. Out of ignorance many believers have sought out new age information and gurus to help them understand their dreams. This is one of the reasons some church leaders completely dismiss the concept of God speaking to man through dreams. Ultimately all information and interpretation of dreams should point us back to God and His Word. Please note that dreams are not a replacement for study of the Word, time in prayer, and intimacy with our Heavenly Father. Every dream is not from God nor does every dream have any type of spiritual benefit.

Visions-3

Vision: an experience of seeing someone or something in a dream or trance, or as a supernatural apparition

Unlike dreams with visions the person is awake. Many times, a vision is quickly dismissed as the imagination run wild or just some odd happenstance. Visions can be powerful but to the novice they can be scary. Like dreams, visions are a visual form of communication that allows you to "see" a message from God. Many people will see visions but they struggle to put spoken words to what they saw. The ability to understand and put language to what is seen in a vision comes from the Holy Spirit.

Very often children will ignore visions because they assume it is their imagination. Many children will see visions and not say anything because they do not want to seem odd or weird. Visions are like dreams in the sense they usually have a strong visual component but instead of being sleep you are awake. By being awake you are less prone to forget what you have seen.

Habakkuk said he would wait to "see" what God is saying. In general, we wait to hear what a person is saying but many times God will show us visually what He is saying at the moment.

> Habakkuk 2:1 "I will stand upon my watch, and set me upon the tower, and will watch to see what he

will say unto me, and what I shall answer when I am reproved."

Divine visions and dreams come from the Lord which means that you cannot pick and choose when they come and what information is received.

Inward Vision and Open Vision

Inward Visions: (Picture an apple in your mind). Inward visions to keep it simple is basically when you are seeing a vision and it is as if you are seeing this in your mind.

Outward Visions/Open Visions: (Look at what is in front of you) Outward visions can be described as seeing a picture placed in front of your face.

Visions are another powerful and unique way that God can communicate with mankind. Visions can intensify through worship and prayer. Visions are a unique way of God revealing speaking a truth to us. All visions are not from God nor do all visions have any spiritual benefit.

Acts 2:17 "And it shall come to pass in the last days, saith God, I will pour out of my Spirit upon all flesh: and your sons and your daughters shall prophesy, and your young men shall see visions, and your old men shall dream dreams:"

Special Communication to Special People-4

One population of people that tend to be left out as it relates to the prophetic is the blind and deaf community or the sensory impaired. They are no less loved by God than anyone else. Therefore, He desires and can speak to them just like the rest of mankind. One thing to understand as it relates to those that are deaf or blind is that the brain has a way of compensating for the loss or lack of function of one's senses. This is why the brain will in a sense re-wire itself in a way that the other senses are enhanced. A person that is sensory impaired will attest to the fact that the other senses are stronger. This is what enables people that are blind to use sound to "see" and they can move around like someone that can see with their two eyes, this technique is known as echolocation. Echolocation is a result of the accommodations the brain has made to adjust to the sensory impairment.

The visually impaired use Braille and the hearing-impaired use sign language to speak because all people are created to communicate with others. When people are unable to communicate with other people learning, social skills, and even mental health will be affected. Have you ever lost your voice and struggled for people to be able to understand what you are saying? The inability to be understood can happen a lot in the Christian community when there is a lack of people that "speak" the language of those that they are trying to communicate with. It is imperative that the faith-based community does not exclude the sensory impaired.

Dreams and the Sensory Impaired (Hearing & Vision)

There have been studies conducted on sensory impaired individuals to help bring insight to what the dream world is like for them. The ability of the brain to compensate for sensory impairments does not exclude dreams. Even though God given dreams are spiritual and will pull on our spiritual senses God is wise enough to keep our abilities the same in our dreams.[2]

If a person went blind during childhood or later in life, they are prone to "seeing" in their dreams and overtime the sight in their dreams will begin to fade. But if a person is born blind they will not see in their dreams. This concept is the same for those that are born deaf or that lose hearing later in life. When it comes to dreams, people that are blind, or visually impaired, are more likely to have dreams with intensified sound, smell, taste, and feeling. Individuals with impairment of sight have shared dreams with strong winds, intense smells and taste, loud booms, and other phenomenon.[2]

---

[2] Michelle Carr, P. (2016, September 30). People With Hearing Loss Have More Vivid Dreams. *Psychology today*. New York, NY, USA.

Depending on whether a person was born deaf or went deaf later in life will dictate whether they "hear" in their dreams. People that are born deaf are not going to "hear" in their dreams. But they tend to have dreams that are visually heightened with bright vivid colors and strong impressions through what they are seeing and feeling. Many people that are hearing impaired have reported dreams where they automatically know what a person was saying in a dream. It is also not uncommon for those with visual and auditory impairment to have heightened smell in their dreams just like in their everyday lives. There is a lot more than can be said but this was just a small amount of information to encourage parents to realize God has not forgotten their child and He can speak to them too!!! As believers, we should be able to connect prophetic children that are sensory impaired back to the Father.

You typically dream in the way you communicate in day to day life. A lot of deaf people that communicate via sign language have dreams where everyone in the dream can sign. There will also be heightened taste, touch, and smell. But for many the visual component of the dream will leave a very strong impression. Others have stated that there is no one talking but you "know" what the people are saying. Unfortunately, many have ascribed this to telepathy because they do not understand the language of God.

I think it is important to realize that in the faith-based community we are overlooking people as if God doesn't speak to them when He does, but in many cases barriers in communication can leave them open to be indoctrinated from a secular humanistic approach. Basically, because most Christians are not fluent in Braille or sign language this population of people are prone to be taught things with no regard for God and His word.

We cannot empower believers and forget those that have sensory impairments. Yes, God can heal but even when Jesus walked the earth, He did not heal everyone and raise everyone from the dead. God wants to raise up people that are visually impaired and auditorily impaired. They will then be able to minister to other people.

The inability to see and hear does not mean a person is deficient in intellect. You can have a sensory impairment and be as smart as Einstein. We should ensure that sensory impaired children are being connected to God so that they are able to minister to those in their community and that surround them. A lot of people with sensory impairments are educated and trained to survive in the earth but many times they are not learning about Jesus or being filled with the Holy Spirit.

Supernatural Encounters-5

Supernatural: A manifestation or event attributed to some force beyond scientific understanding or the laws of nature

Night Terrors

Many prophetic children go through an intense season of demonic harassment. This can include frequent nightmares with witches, owls, spiders and so forth. A lot of prophetic children also deal with demonic spirits manifesting themselves to the point they can be seen and felt. This can be quite stressful and upsetting for children. This happens a lot because prophetic children are very different and sometimes, they are recognized by hell before they are recognized by their parents or even their spiritual leaders.

We must be wise in realizing that some of these demonic encounters are caused by doors being open through entertainment (toys, movies, music, books) or even through curiosity and ignorance (psychic hotlines, tea leaves, palm reading, Ouija boards, tarot cards, crystals, white magic). If you know or even believe your child has opened a door for demons to have legal grounds in their lives there must be renunciation and repentance.

For many children, these demonic encounters can cause fear that can last a lifetime. There are a lot of adults that love God but are terrified by the dark or that continue to have nightmares because of the root of fear in their lives.

Imaginary Friends

One of the easier ways the enemy likes to gain access to small children is through familiar spirits disguised as a deceased relative or even a friend that can only be seen by them. When children make the mistake of engaging with these demons in disguise it can cause issues even in their adult years. The only spirit anyone should be communicating with is the Holy Spirit. So, when these demons have access to communicate with children, they can subtly lead them astray towards a path of destruction. This can also cause children to become socially awkward as they lack the ability to build normal healthy friendships because they have spent so much time with their imaginary friends.

After a while many children want their imaginary friend to stop talking but this does not happen automatically. It takes the power of God to break these demonic alliances. When the voices and irate behaviors escalate often this can eventually lead to mental health treatment and diagnoses. It is imperative as parents that we keep our children covered spiritually and that we are always spiritual watchmen in their lives.

Angels

It is not uncommon for children to sense and discern that angels are in their midst. And some children can outright see in the spirit that angels are in the room or near them. There are many prophetically gifted people that can "see" in the spirit. Shockingly "seeing" in the spirit can be easier is easier for children because they are not tainted. Many adults have been tainted by polluting themselves from using their eyes to view vile things such as pornography.

> Psalms 101:3 "I will set no wicked thing before mine eyes: I hate the work of them that turn aside; it shall not cleave to me."

Baptism of the Holy Spirit

There is no junior Holy Spirit. Our children can receive the baptism of the Holy Spirit just like we can. As parents, we have to desire for our children to be filled with the evidence of speaking in tongues. The baptism of the Holy Spirit is the gateway to the manifestation of spiritual gifts and a new depth in God. We can help prepare our children to receive the baptism of the Holy Spirit by teaching them the Word of God and praying with them.

> Acts 2:4 "And they were all filled with the Holy Ghost, and began to speak with other tongues, as the Spirit gave them utterance."

> Acts 19:6 "And when Paul had laid his hands upon them, the Holy Ghost came on them; and they spake with tongues, and prophesied."

Whether it is a dream, vision or supernatural encounter as parents we need to be open to listen to our children. This will allow us to recognize if they are receiving communication from God or even demonic sources.

D'Andrea M. Bolden

Tips and Tools for Dreams-6

Combatting Nightmares
Below are a few tips to help children that are battling nightmares
1. Pray for and with your children. It is important that you pray for your children at night as well as in the home and even in their rooms and especially their closets.

2. Ensure nothing is fueling these encounters. It is imperative to ensure there are no TV shows, cultural items (art), movies, toys, games, books etc., that have elements of the occult.

3. Teach them how to pray. Teach your children the power of the blood of Jesus Christ and how to pray when these situations occur.

4. Explain that what is happening is not of God. Because demons will try and communicate with children ensure they are not entertaining imaginary or invisible friends.

5. Fill them with the Word of God. Take the time to read and study the Word of God with your children.

Unlocking the dream world
A few tips to help with the dream world. What we see in our dreams are all pieces and components that make up a huge language. There are a lot of great resources out there that focus on the topic of dreams and interpretation from a strong

biblical perspective. Many resources will give a strong biblical foundation and reference scripture to help explain dream interpretation. I just wanted to personally list a few things in this book.

Location: The location of a dream is very important. The location can indicate a lot that the Lord is conveying in a dream.

1. Bathroom: A place of cleansing (repentance) and preparation
2. Old place of residence: Dealing with the past or a former and familiar situation.
3. School: Training, learning, natural (school), education and academics.

Activities: The things that you are doing in a dream are very important. Your activity or what you are doing in a dream can be a major component.

1. Swimming (strong): Worship or flowing in the gifts of the spirit
2. Swimming (drowning): Feeling overwhelmed, in over your head, or even depression.

Emotions: The emotions you feel in your dream are relevant. Did you feel angry, happy, or even scared? The emotions in your dream say a lot about how it affected your innermost being.

Other things to consider are other people in the dream, sounds, vehicles, clothing, hair, numbers, animals, leaders (secular or spiritual), money and so forth.

There are a lot of BIBLICALLY based books that teach extensively on dream interpretation. They break down the various elements of dreams and give a scripture reference for each one. Ultimately, our number one source and guide should always be the God and His Word.

… Raising Prophets & Prophetic Types

Parent & Kid Devotion Day 1
-Baptism of the Holy Spirit-

Who is the Holy Spirit? The Holy Spirit is not an "it" or a thing but He is God in the form of His power. As followers of Jesus Christ, the Holy Spirit plays a very important role in our spiritual walk with the Lord. Because Jesus is our Lord and Savior, He desires to empower us and this happens by baptizing us with the Holy Ghost. The baptism of the Holy Ghost just means that we are filled up with the Spirit of God. The baptism of the Holy Spirit is an overflow or abundance of God's spirit. A visual depiction of this would be to take an empty cup and fill it water and keep pouring water even after the cup has filled and the water is spilling outside of the cup. The baptism of the Holy Spirit happens when we welcome Him to use our vessel as a place of residence for God's power. Did you know that your body is the temple of the Holy Ghost? (See I Corinthians 6:19). The Holy Ghost is what gives us the ability to do what God has created us to do. For you to receive the gift of the Holy Ghost all you must do is ask and believe that you will receive this precious gift. Without the Holy Spirit, we will never experience the fullness of God.

>**John 7:37-39** "In the last day, that great day of the feast, Jesus stood and cried, saying, If any man thirst, let him come unto me, and drink. [38] He that believeth on me, as the scripture hath said, out of his belly shall flow rivers of living water. [39] (But this spake he of the Spirit, which they that believe on him should receive:

for the Holy Ghost was not yet given; because that Jesus was not yet glorified.)"

Acts 1:8 "But ye shall receive power, after that the Holy Ghost is come upon you: and ye shall be witnesses unto me both in Jerusalem, and in all Judaea, and in Samaria, and unto the uttermost part of the earth."

John 16:7 "Nevertheless I tell you the truth; It is expedient for you that I go away: for if I go not away, the Comforter will not come unto you; but if I depart, I will send him unto you."

Acts 2:4 "And they were all filled with the Holy Ghost, and began to speak with other tongues, as the Spirit gave them utterance."

Acts 19:6 "And when Paul had laid his hands upon them, the Holy Ghost came on them; and they spake with tongues, and prophesied."

1. Ask God to baptize you with His Holy Spirit. Take a moment and just ask God for the precious gift of the Holy Spirit.

2. Believe and receive by faith

**Having faith and believing when you are praying to receive the baptism of the Holy Spirit is very important. God moves according to our faith. Everything we receive from God is by faith!!

Parent & Kid Devotion Day 2
-Prophetic Activation - Write what you hear-

Here are the 4 Keys to Activating Your Child in the Prophetic

1. Any child desiring to prophesy should be Spirit filled because the baptism of the Holy Spirit is the prerequisite **[Acts 19:6]**. (See Day 1)

2. Take the time to explain and define prophecy to your child. [Simple definition: Prophecy is speaking and revealing God's heart and will for a specific persons(s) or place(s).] Consider the age and level of maturity because sometimes simpler works best. Be sure to explain things at a level that is appropriate for your child. Just explain the basics no need to go too far in depth right away especially with younger children. It is better to let them grow in their prophetic grace and continue teaching them as they grow to avoid overwhelming them. Make sure they understand that prophecy should build, exhort and edify God's people and is not to be used to cause harm in any sort of way.

But he that prophesieth speaketh unto men to edification, and exhortation, and comfort. -- **I Corinthians 14:3**

3. Ensure that they understand that they can PROPHESY [I Corinthians 14:31]. I have found that children can be a bit fearful, bashful or just unsure but most of the time they are willing so be sure to reiterate that they CAN PROPHESY.

I would that ye all spake with tongues, but rather that ye prophesied: for greater is he that prophesieth than he that speaketh with tongues, except he interpret, that the church may receive edifying. **I Corinthians 14:5**

For you can all prophesy in turn so that everyone may be instructed and encouraged. **I Corinthians 14:31**

4. Activate their faith and allow them to begin to share what God is saying to them. Times of prayer and quiet times of reading the Word are great opportunities to activate your child in the prophetic. Their ability to hear can be hindered for a number of reasons. They must learn how to quiet down and take the time to receive what the Holy Spirit is releasing to their Spirit. Some children will "see" the Word of the Lord in images, visions, words etc., while others may primarily hear the Word of the Lord and this is totally normal.
Exercise #1: [Simple prophetic word] Have your child pray and ask the Holy Spirit to speak one single word to them and then have them share what He is saying
Exercise # 2 This is another simple exercise to help your child record what the Holy Spirit is saying to you.

1. Listen to the voice of the Holy Spirit
2. Write down what you hear on the next page

What you hear can be as simple as one word. This is a simple exercise that will increase your faith and help fine tune your ears.

Be sure to continue to build your child's faith and encourage them to desire to prophesy. It is important for them to understand the role faith plays in regard to prophecy. They must have faith and believe that God will use them to prophesy. Ultimately our level of faith can affect our prophetic abilities.

Wherefore, brethren, covet to prophesy, and forbid not to speak with tongues. ***I Corinthians 14:39***

Having then gifts differing according to the grace that is given to us, whether prophecy, let us prophesy according to the proportion of faith; ***[Romans 12:6]***

D'Andrea M. Bolden

Parent & Kid Devotion Day 3

-Record a Recent Dream or Vision-

Encourage and help your child record a recent dream that they have had and include as many details as possible.

Date:

Location:

People:

Colors:

Numbers:

Animals:

Emotions felt:

Activities (i.e. singing, walking, driving etc.,)

Summary of the dream:
_____
_____
_____
_____
_____
_____
_____
_____

… Raising Prophets & Prophetic Types

Parent & Kid Devotion Day 4
-Prayer Exercise-

1. Explain to them what prayer is as well as God's purpose for prayer. Prayer is a vehicle that allows us to communicate with our heavenly prayer. Prayer is the medium that allows us to verbally release God's will in the earth.

2. Let them hear you pray out loud.
It is important that our children hear and see us active in prayer. As parents, our greatest audience is our children and we must lead by example.

3. Pray with them but encourage them to begin to lead in prayer. As children are learning to pray it is important to pray with them and as they become more comfortable allow them to begin "leading" in prayer and taking more of a lead role. This will build their confidence and it allows them to learn to pray with a greater level of independence.

4. Show them in the Word what God says about prayer.
It is always important to know what God's word says about a matter. Because prayer is such an important part of our walk as believers that are plenty of scriptures about prayer. Listed below are several scriptural passages on prayer.

> **Philippians 4:6** "Be careful for nothing; but in every thing by prayer and supplication with thanksgiving let your requests be made known unto God."

Mark 11:24 "Therefore I say unto you, What things soever ye desire, when ye pray, believe that ye receive [them], and ye shall have [them]."

1 Thessalonians 5:17 "Pray without ceasing."

Matthew 6:7 "But when ye pray, use not vain repetitions, as the heathen [do]: for they think that they shall be heard for their much speaking."

Matthew 26:41 "Watch and pray, that ye enter not into temptation: the spirit indeed [is] willing, but the flesh [is] weak."

James 5:16 'Confess [your] faults one to another, and pray one for another, that ye may be healed. The effectual fervent prayer of a righteous man availeth much."

Jeremiah 33:3 "Call unto me, and I will answer thee, and shew thee great and mighty things, which thou knowest not."

Ephesians 6:18 "Praying always with all prayer and supplication in the Spirit, and watching thereunto with all perseverance and supplication for all saints;"

Luke 18:1 "And he spake a parable unto them [to this end], that men ought always to pray, and not to faint

<u>Try this using the scripture below</u>

For I know the plans I have for you," declares the LORD, "plans to prosper you and not to harm you, plans to give you hope and a future – **Jeremiah 29:11**

5. Allow them room to pray about what is in their heart.
I can remember when my daughter was younger, she would pray for Dora, Back Yardigans and any other cartoon pal she

could think of because at that age she did not know any better. This type of behavior is normal for younger children. Now that she is older she knows to pray for things that are appropriate and realistic and because she knows the voice of the Lord she is sensitive enough to be more led by His Spirit in prayer.

The Lord desires for our children to seek Him and know Him from the place of prayer.

Exercise # 1: [Accelerated Prayer] You can do this with either just you and your children or with a small group. The goal is to have each person pray around a prayer point (family, protection, healing etc.) for about 20 seconds and then go on to the next person do this a few times to allow each person the opportunity to pray multiple times.

This will allow them a chance to pray in a group and become more confident. It will also teach them how to pray with focus by having a prayer point.

Exercise # 2: Pick a simple scripture that is easy for them to understand and show them how to pray the Word of God back to the Father. When we pray God's word, we echo back to him what he has already spoken, we also add more authority and strength to our prayer. Praying God's word allows us to agree with what He has already spoken.

D'Andrea M. Bolden

Parent & Kid Devotion Day 5
-Prophetic Activation - Draw What You See-

This is an exercise geared toward the young prophetic artist. Because prophetic artists are very creative and can be quite spontaneous. This is a simple exercise to help your child "create" what the Holy Spirit is showing them.

1. Always emphasize the important of your child being led by and listening to the voice of the Holy Spirit. For this exercise feel free to use any of the following:
    a. Previous Dream or Previous Vision
    b. Current Vision Draw, paint or even creatively re-create what God has shown you previously or at this very moment.

Section 4

Prophetic children: Innovators, Inventors + Entrepreneurs

Innovation - 1

in·no·va·tion - /ˌinəˈvāSH(ə)n/

(noun) 1. the introduction of something new, 2. a new idea, method, or device
Ref: https://www.merriam-webster.com/dictionary/innovation

> In the beginning, God created the heavens and the earth. – **Genesis 1:1**

We serve the God of creation and He created the universe and everything in it because He is the greatest innovator. The creative and innovative nature of God is what allows us to also be innovative. Although we are all created in His image some people are stronger in some areas than others. For example, some people are very innovative and they are always working on creating something new or the next big thing.

> And, "You, Lord, laid the foundation of the earth in the beginning, and the heavens are the work of your hands;- **Hebrews 1:10**

Prophetically gifted children have a high tendency to be extremely visual and very innovative by nature. The ability to couple natural talents and abilities with the prophetic gives believers an advantage. Prophetic children tend to stand out in the areas that they are strongest. They very easily show extraordinary abilities but sometimes these abilities are overlooked if they come in an unexpected or unconventional way. A great example would be how some parents can very early on recognize athletic abilities and musical talents in their children. While many other parents can easily overlook or not recognize that their child is an innovator or entrepreneur.

Often times the ability and desire of our children to be innovative can be fed or killed by parents and their environment. If they are told their ideas are stupid, or to stop using their imagination or if they are constantly laughed at or even ignored they might stop trying to be innovative.

People that are innovators are many times the force behind new trends, inventions, medical research technological breakthroughs, scientific advancements, cutting-edge business models, and other new things that are manifesting in the earth.

Science + Research

Prophetic children that are innovative work well in the scientific community. In fact, a number of technological, scientific, and medical breakthroughs were derived from a dream. Now all of these people that had dreams were not believers but how much more can God download into those that are His and that know His voice. I can remember when I was a child spending time in the kitchen mixing my mother's seasonings together expecting them to go boom. So, it is probably not a surprise that I studied chemistry in college. Prophetic people can be great assets even as it relates to research because many times, they see what others do not.

D'Andrea M. Bolden

Inventions + Dreams - 2

in·ven·tion - /inˈven(t)SH(ə)n/

noun 1. the action of inventing something, typically a process or device:
Ref: https://www.merriam-webster.com/dictionary/invention

A lot of dreamers are responsible for some of the world's greatest inventions. There are countless stories about inventions that were created after the concept was revealed in a dream. Sadly, a lot of these individuals are oblivious to the fact the source of not all but some of these powerful dreams was God. When we read the bible, we can see that God has always used dreams and visions to communicate with man. Many times, when God begins to "awaken" prophetic people they begin to have dreams and visions. In fact, a lot of prophetic children have strong dreams and visions early on in life. Through these dreams and visions come art, songs, business ideas, books, poetry, new designs, cutting edge ideas and even scientific breakthroughs. I personally have had dreams about songs, inventions, businesses, as well as books.

1. Madame C.J. Walker had issues with her hair falling out. In a dream it was revealed to her what ingredient to mix up and put in her hair. To her surprise not only did it work but her hair was growing in very fast. She decided to sell this as a product and she eventually became the first black millionaire in America.

2. Elias Howe had an issue with creating an operable sewing machine. In a dream he saw what he needed to do in order to solve the problem he had with the needle. This allowed him to create an operable sewing machine.

3. Robert Louis Stevenson is the author of Dr. Jekyll and Mr. Hyde. He describes how he writes these books as the plot comes to him in a series of dreams. Robert stated that his dreams were very vivid and entertaining and that he dreamed about an entire storyline for a book.

4. Srinivasa Ramanujan was a mathematical genius who would get insight and even new formulas in his dreams. Sometimes he would see a handwriting and he would get up and verify the formulas that he was in his dream. He discovered the infinite series of pi. He had little to no formal training in math but states his success is related to his dreams.

5. Stephen King is a world-renown author and he shared how his inspiration for writing Misery and other books came to him in a dream.

6. Larry Page is known for creating an invention based on a dream and this invention that is used heavily around the world is Google.

7. Friedrich August Kekulé von Stradonitz is a figure in the history of chemistry and he discovered that shape of benzene unlike many other molecules was not linear. This discovery came to him in a dream. This breakthrough was monumental for the world of chemistry.

8. Dmitry Mendeleyev saw the entire periodic table in a dream. After work tirelessly for several days he took a quick break to nap. While he was asleep, he saw a table with all the elements arranged properly. He quickly recorded this, and it was a major contribution to the world of chemistry.

9. Dr. James Watson had a dream that helped brining understanding to the structure of DNA. He had a dream that caused him to consider that double helix as the structure for DNA.

10. Niehls Bohr had a dream that revealed the structure of the atom. He saw electrons spinning around the atom. After having this dream he was confident it was correct. But he performed testing to verify that this was in fact accurate and true. He later received a Nobel prize.

11. Otto Loewi had a dream about an experiment that showed him that nerve impulses were not electrical but chemical. He is also responsible for the discovery of acetylcholine. Acetylcholine is the neurotransmitter that promotes dreaming. He was eventually awarded a Nobel prize.

Chapter References

Conradt, S. (2012, October 11). *Mental Floss*. Retrieved from Mental Floss: http://mentalfloss.com/article/12763/11-creative-breakthroughs-people-had-their-sleep might make great cupcakes, or maybe they have formulated some great perfume or nail polish.

Prophetic children that are strong innovators can sometimes make great entrepreneurs. A lot of prophetic children that are creative and innovative have a hard time fitting into the rigid jobs in corporate America as adults. For some prophetic children creating and innovating is easy but taking their passion and their gifts and making it profitable can be more difficult. Sometimes creatives can be very unorganized as they follow their creativity from one idea to another. Discipline and consistency and focus is needed for entrepreneurs that are strong creatives. They are prone to get bored and will be ready to jump to the next idea. This is not altogether bad but in order for the business to become successful a team of people will have to help manage the company. This will allow them to focus on what they are passionate about and that is innovating, inventing, and being creative.

Some kidpreneurs are more focused on building a robust well-run organization or even generating a profit. These are the type of entrepreneurs that have the focus, patience and follow through needed to build an empire from the ground up. They are strong visionaries that "see" the potential of what their business can become. They are confident in their products or services that they offer and they are willing to put in the work to succeed. Although they might not be as creativity driven as others, they are still cutting edge. No matter what their strength or focus in entrepreneurship it is important to allow them to grow in their role and become confident.

Children that are stronger as innovators and inventors might not be as interested in the actual aspects of running and growing the business. In many cases they simply prefer being free to create. On the other hand, some children are not strong inventors, but they might have the ability to be a strong innovator and problem solver. They might even create a business that is a solution to a problem. Like with many other gifts and talents some children can easily be identified as entrepreneurs (kidpreneurs) they are constantly trying to create and sell products (i.e. lemonade, art, beauty supplies, food etc.). They have the strong desire to be a boss and have clear vision and passion. While in other children it might not be as obvious.

Ultimately allow them to have fun and realize some children take more time to grow into their role. Some mature and become more focused a little later and that is fine. Just keep nurturing and sowing seeds. Send them to camps, find books for them to read, even find a business mentor for them. There are a number of events and online hubs for kidpreneurs. As a parent take the time to find avenues to invest in this area of your child's life.

Section 5

Bright Idea

Does your child have ideas for inventions, books, songs, webinars, or even a business? I find that children are full of creativity and a lot of great ideas. Use the next few pages to help organize your child's idea. Then put together actions steps to get your child's idea moving forward and off the ground.

D'Andrea M. Bolden

Bright Idea

Think Tank Brainstorming – Idea Overload

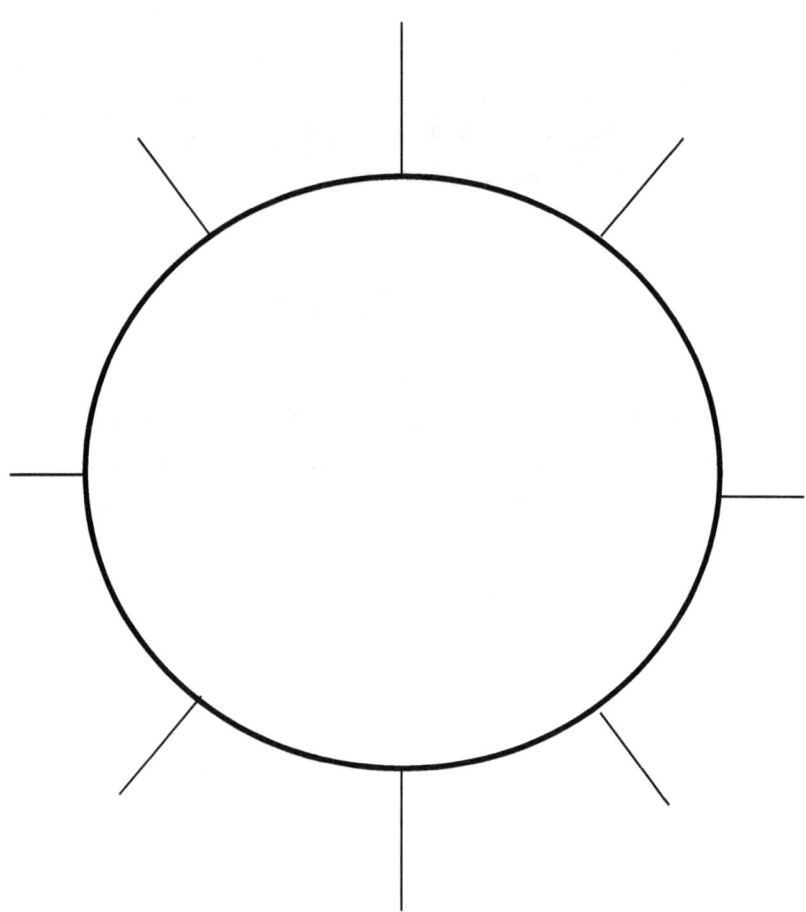

Bright Idea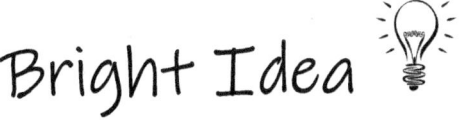

Invention

Describe your idea:
_____
_____
_____
_____

Does this idea require experts? (i.e. engineers, coder, app designers etc.)
_____
_____

Will you need a trademark, patent or even both?
_____
_____
_____

Will you need a prototype?
_____
_____

Things to consider:

- ✓ Protecting your invention with patents and trademarks
- ✓ Legal advice to understand any state, federal and industry related regulations.
- ✓ Lawyer to handle patent/trademark application
- ✓ A company that can create a prototype if needed for your particular invention.
- ✓ Researching a legit company that can manufacture your product if this is necessary.
- ✓ Creating a legal business entity for when you are ready to put your product on the market.
- ✓ Professional graphics and packaging
- ✓ Costs involved to get started
- ✓ Will you need investors or a business loan?

Business Idea

Business Name:

_____
_____
_____

List of Products/Services

1. _____
2. _____
3. _____
4. _____
5. _____

Target Market:

_____
_____
_____

How will your business operate (online, physical location, pop-ups, or a combination)? Be specific.

_____
_____
_____

Things to consider:

- ✓ Business Plan and confidentiality forms
- ✓ Full branding (logo, website, business cards, business email, fonts, typography, social media platforms etc.)
- ✓ Professional photos of your kidpreneur
- ✓ Packaging (if applicable)
- ✓ Business phone number and voice mail
- ✓ Business press kit
- ✓ Press Release
- ✓ General liability insurance
- ✓ Distribution (if applicable)
- ✓ Costs involved to get started
- ✓ Will you need investors or a business loan?

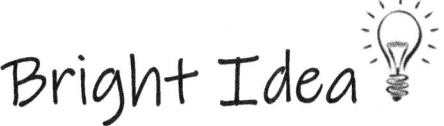

Other Idea

What is your idea (book, song, webinar, podcast, etc.)

_____

_____

Title/Name

_____

_____

Do you need to copyright your idea?

_____

_____

If your idea is a book, song, podcast or audio-visual content how will you make it available to people? (CD baby, amazon, iTunes, YouTube, iBooks etc)

_____

_____

If your idea **is** a webinar, online class etc. what platform will you use to make this available (zoom, gotowebinar etc.)?

_____

_____

Things to Consider

- ✓ Costs to protect intellectual property (copyrights)
- ✓ Options to distribute things such as books, podcasts, and music
- ✓ Platforms to host online class or webinar and the costs involved
- ✓ Professional graphics and branding
- ✓ Does your idea require you setting up a state registered business entity (LLC, S-Corp, etc)

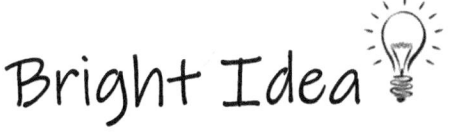

Action Steps - Introduction

On the next page you are going to list the steps that are needed to get your child's idea from paper to manifestation. Consider everything that is needed to get the vision moving forward. If necessary, use google to find online blogs and other resources that can tell you what you will need for your child's specific idea. There is a surplus of free information on topics such as; book publishing, how to launch a clothing line, or even how to start a podcast. Once you have all the details you will then put together your action steps and include deadlines to keep you on schedule. It is a good idea to continuously update your action steps so that the idea does not fall to the ground or become idle. Once you set up your social media account how will you continuously create and update content? What is your marketing plan? These are things to consider to help keep the dream alive so to speak.

Here are a few examples of possible action steps that are not necessarily relevant to you and are not in a particular order.

1 Register business with the state
2 Get EIN from IRS
3 Set up business banking account
       Will need business incorporation documents
       Will need business EIN
4 Professionally designed business logo
5 Professionally designed website

D'Andrea M. Bolden

Bright Idea

Action Steps

1
_____

2
_____

3
_____

4
_____

5
_____

6
_____

7
_____

8

_____

9

_____

10

_____

11

_____

12

_____

13

_____

14

_____

15

_____

D'Andrea M. Bolden

Section 6

Dream Journal

Raising Prophets & Prophetic Types

Dream Topic: _____

Date: _____

Dream Details:

D'Andrea M. Bolden

Dream Topic: _____

Date: _____

Dream Details:

_____
_____
_____
_____
_____
_____
_____
_____
_____
_____
_____
_____
_____
_____
_____
_____
_____
_____
_____
_____
_____
_____
_____
_____

Raising Prophets & Prophetic Types

Dream Topic: _____

Date: _____

Dream Details:

D'Andrea M. Bolden

Dream Topic: _____

Date: _____

Dream Details:

_____
_____
_____
_____
_____
_____
_____
_____
_____
_____
_____
_____
_____
_____
_____
_____
_____
_____
_____
_____
_____
_____
_____
_____
_____
_____
_____

Raising Prophets & Prophetic Types

Dream Topic: _____

Date: _____

Dream Details:

Dream Topic: _____

Date: _____

Dream Details:

Raising Prophets & Prophetic Types

Dream Topic: _____

Date: _____

Dream Details:

Dream Topic: _____

Date: _____

Dream Details:

Raising Prophets & Prophetic Types

Dream Topic: _____

Date: _____

Dream Details:

D'Andrea M. Bolden

Dream Topic: _____

Date: _____

Dream Details:

Raising Prophets & Prophetic Types

Dream Topic: _____

Date: _____

Dream Details:

D'Andrea M. Bolden

Dream Topic: _____

Date: _____

Dream Details:

Raising Prophets & Prophetic Types

Dream Topic: _____

Date: _____

Dream Details:

D'Andrea M. Bolden

Dream Topic: _____

Date: _____

Dream Details:

_____
_____
_____
_____
_____
_____
_____
_____
_____
_____
_____
_____
_____
_____
_____
_____
_____
_____
_____
_____
_____
_____
_____
_____
_____
_____
_____
_____
_____
_____
_____

Raising Prophets & Prophetic Types

Dream Topic: _____

Date: _____

Dream Details:

_____
_____
_____
_____
_____
_____
_____
_____
_____
_____
_____
_____
_____
_____
_____
_____
_____
_____
_____
_____
_____
_____
_____
_____
_____

D'Andrea M. Bolden

Dream Topic: _____

Date: _____

Dream Details:

Raising Prophets & Prophetic Types

Dream Topic: _____

Date: _____

Dream Details:

Dream Topic: _____

Date: _____

Dream Details:

Raising Prophets & Prophetic Types

Dream Topic: _____

Date: _____

Dream Details:

Dream Topic: _____

Date: _____

Dream Details:

_____
_____
_____
_____
_____
_____
_____
_____
_____
_____
_____
_____
_____
_____
_____
_____
_____
_____
_____
_____
_____
_____
_____
_____
_____
_____
_____

Raising Prophets & Prophetic Types

Dream Topic: _____

Date: _____

Dream Details:

D'Andrea M. Bolden

Dream Topic: _____

Date: _____

Dream Details:

_____
_____
_____
_____
_____
_____
_____
_____
_____
_____
_____
_____
_____
_____
_____
_____
_____
_____
_____
_____
_____
_____
_____
_____
_____

Raising Prophets & Prophetic Types

Dream Topic: _____

Date: _____

Dream Details:

D'Andrea M. Bolden

Dream Topic: _____

Date: _____

Dream Details:

_____
_____
_____
_____
_____
_____
_____
_____
_____
_____
_____
_____
_____
_____
_____
_____
_____
_____
_____
_____
_____
_____
_____
_____
_____
_____
_____
_____

Raising Prophets & Prophetic Types

Dream Topic: _____

Date: _____

Dream Details:

Dream Topic: _____

Date: _____

Dream Details:

Raising Prophets & Prophetic Types

Dream Topic: _____

Date: _____

Dream Details:

D'Andrea M. Bolden

Dream Topic: _____

Date: _____

Dream Details:

_____
_____
_____
_____
_____
_____
_____
_____
_____
_____
_____
_____
_____
_____
_____
_____
_____
_____
_____
_____
_____
_____
_____
_____
_____
_____
_____

Raising Prophets & Prophetic Types

Dream Topic: _____

Date: _____

Dream Details:

D'Andrea M. Bolden

Dream Topic: _____

Date: _____

Dream Details:

_____
_____
_____
_____
_____
_____
_____
_____
_____
_____
_____
_____
_____
_____
_____
_____
_____
_____
_____
_____
_____
_____
_____
_____
_____
_____
_____
_____

Raising Prophets & Prophetic Types

Dream Topic: _____

Date: _____

Dream Details:

_____
_____
_____
_____
_____
_____
_____
_____
_____
_____
_____
_____
_____
_____
_____
_____
_____
_____
_____
_____
_____
_____
_____
_____
_____

D'Andrea M. Bolden

Dream Topic: _____

Date: _____

Dream Details:

Raising Prophets & Prophetic Types

Dream Topic: _____

Date: _____

Dream Details:

D'Andrea M. Bolden

Dream Topic: _____

Date: _____

Dream Details:

_____
_____
_____
_____
_____
_____
_____
_____
_____
_____
_____
_____
_____
_____
_____
_____
_____
_____
_____
_____
_____
_____
_____
_____
_____
_____
_____
_____

www.ingramcontent.com/pod-product-compliance
Lightning Source LLC
Chambersburg PA
CBHW070546010526
44118CB00012B/1244